# Wai Wai Nu

*Fighting for LGBTQ Rights in Myanmar – Unauthorized*

Emeka Oluwaseun

*ISBN: 9781779695871*
*Imprint: Telephasic Workshop*
Copyright © 2024 Emeka Oluwaseun.
All Rights Reserved.

# Contents

# Growing Up in a Traditional Society

Growing up in a traditional society like Myanmar poses unique challenges, especially for individuals who identify as LGBTQ. This section explores the complexities of navigating one's identity within the confines of cultural expectations, familial pressures, and societal norms that often marginalize those who do not conform to heteronormative standards.

## 1.1.1 Early Childhood in Yangon

Wai Wai Nu's early childhood in Yangon was marked by the vibrant yet conservative fabric of Burmese society. The bustling streets were filled with the sounds of street vendors, the scents of local cuisine, and the warmth of community life. However, beneath this lively exterior lay a rigid adherence to traditional values that dictated behavior, relationships, and identity.

## 1.1.2 The Influence of Burmese Culture

Burmese culture, steeped in Buddhist teachings and patriarchal structures, emphasized conformity and adherence to societal norms. The teachings of Buddhism often promote compassion and understanding, yet cultural interpretations can lead to exclusionary practices against those who diverge from the accepted norms. This duality creates a complex landscape for individuals like Wai Wai Nu, who felt the pull of cultural heritage while grappling with their emerging identity.

## 1.1.3 Prejudices and Discrimination

Prejudices against LGBTQ individuals are deeply entrenched in Myanmar's traditional society. Discrimination manifests in various forms, from verbal harassment to systemic exclusion from social and economic opportunities. The pervasive belief that homosexuality is a Western import further alienates LGBTQ individuals, as they are often viewed as deviating from the "true" Burmese identity. This societal stigma can lead to internalized homophobia, where individuals struggle to reconcile their identity with societal expectations.

## 1.1.4 A Fearful Secret

For many LGBTQ individuals in Myanmar, including Wai Wai Nu, the fear of being discovered can be paralyzing. The need to conceal one's true self to avoid ostracism or violence creates an environment of secrecy and shame. This fear is compounded by the lack of supportive resources and safe spaces, forcing individuals to navigate their identities in isolation. The internal conflict between authenticity and societal acceptance can lead to significant mental health challenges, including anxiety and depression.

### 1.1.5 The Beginnings of Activism

Despite the oppressive environment, Wai Wai Nu's early experiences sparked the beginnings of activism. Witnessing the injustices faced by LGBTQ individuals ignited a passion for change. The realization that others shared similar struggles fostered a sense of community and purpose. This early activism was characterized by small acts of defiance, such as participating in discussions about gender and sexuality within trusted circles, laying the groundwork for more organized efforts in the future.

### 1.1.6 Finding Support in Unexpected Places

Support often comes from unexpected sources. Wai Wai Nu found solace in friendships with like-minded individuals who also challenged traditional norms. These connections provided a safe haven where they could express their true selves without fear of judgment. The solidarity among peers created a network of support that was crucial for emotional resilience and empowerment.

### 1.1.7 Navigating School and Society

School, a microcosm of society, presented its own set of challenges. The rigid adherence to traditional values often permeated the educational environment, where bullying and discrimination were rampant. For Wai Wai Nu, navigating this landscape required a delicate balance of authenticity and self-preservation. The experience of being different in a conformist setting highlighted the need for inclusive education that recognizes and respects diversity.

### 1.1.8 Discovering the LGBTQ Community

The discovery of the LGBTQ community was a transformative moment for Wai Wai Nu. It provided a sense of belonging and understanding that had been absent in their earlier experiences. Engaging with others who shared similar struggles fostered a sense of identity and purpose. This newfound community became a vital source of strength, offering resources, mentorship, and a collective voice for advocacy.

### 1.1.9 The Impact of Religion

Religion plays a significant role in shaping attitudes towards LGBTQ individuals in Myanmar. While Buddhism espouses values of compassion, the interpretation of religious teachings can often lead to exclusion. The tension between spiritual beliefs and sexual identity can create a profound internal struggle. For Wai Wai Nu, reconciling their identity with religious expectations posed significant challenges, prompting a search for inclusive interpretations of spirituality that embrace diversity.

In conclusion, growing up in a traditional society like Myanmar presents formidable challenges for LGBTQ individuals. The interplay of cultural, familial, and religious influences creates a complex landscape that requires resilience and courage. Wai Wai Nu's journey reflects the struggles and triumphs of many who seek to carve out a space for their identities in a society that often resists change. The early experiences of fear, secrecy, and eventual activism set the stage for a lifelong commitment to fighting for LGBTQ rights in Myanmar.

## Growing Up in a Traditional Society

In Myanmar, a country rich in cultural heritage and traditional values, the experience of growing up in a traditional society can be both beautiful and challenging. The societal norms, deeply rooted in history and religion, shape the lives of individuals from a young age, creating a complex landscape for those who identify as LGBTQ. This section explores the multifaceted nature of growing up in such a society, focusing on the influences of culture, religion, and the pervasive prejudices that often lead to a fearful existence for many LGBTQ individuals.

### 1.1.1 Early Childhood in Yangon

Wai Wai Nu's early childhood in Yangon was marked by vibrant street life, bustling markets, and the sounds of traditional Burmese music. The city, known for its rich tapestry of cultures, offered a unique backdrop for her formative years. However, beneath the surface of this lively environment lay the rigid expectations imposed by a traditional society. Families often held conservative views regarding gender roles and sexuality, which began to shape Wai Wai's understanding of herself and her place in the world.

## 1.1.2 The Influence of Burmese Culture

Burmese culture is steeped in traditions that emphasize familial loyalty, respect for elders, and adherence to societal norms. This cultural framework can create a nurturing environment; however, it also enforces conformity. The expectations to marry, have children, and adhere to traditional gender roles were omnipresent. For LGBTQ individuals, these cultural imperatives can lead to internal conflict, as they grapple with the desire to live authentically while fearing rejection from their families and communities.

## 1.1.3 Prejudices and Discrimination

Prejudices against LGBTQ individuals are prevalent in Myanmar, often fueled by a lack of understanding and the influence of conservative religious teachings. Discrimination manifests in various forms, from subtle social ostracism to overt acts of violence. The stigma surrounding homosexuality is deeply entrenched, making it difficult for individuals to express their identities openly. Research shows that societal attitudes towards LGBTQ individuals are often shaped by cultural myths and misconceptions, leading to a pervasive climate of fear and silence.

## 1.1.4 A Fearful Secret

For many LGBTQ individuals, including Wai Wai, the need to conceal their true selves becomes a survival mechanism. This fear of exposure is compounded by the potential for familial rejection and societal backlash. The internalized homophobia that can arise from such a fearful existence often leads to mental health challenges, including anxiety and depression. The struggle to maintain a facade while yearning for authenticity can be an isolating experience.

## 1.1.5 The Beginnings of Activism

Despite the challenges, Wai Wai's early experiences also sowed the seeds of her future activism. The injustices she witnessed and experienced ignited a passion for change. As she began to understand the broader implications of discrimination, she sought out like-minded individuals who shared her vision for a more inclusive society. This early engagement with activism laid the groundwork for her future efforts in advocating for LGBTQ rights in Myanmar.

### 1.1.6 Finding Support in Unexpected Places

In a society that often marginalizes LGBTQ voices, finding support can be a daunting task. However, Wai Wai discovered that solidarity could emerge from unexpected places. Through informal networks and underground gatherings, she connected with others who understood her struggles. These relationships became crucial in fostering a sense of community and belonging, providing the emotional support necessary to navigate the complexities of her identity.

### 1.1.7 Navigating School and Society

Navigating the educational system in Myanmar posed its own challenges for Wai Wai. Schools often reflect the broader societal attitudes towards LGBTQ individuals, which can result in bullying and discrimination. The pressure to conform to traditional gender roles within the school environment heightened her sense of alienation. Yet, these experiences also fueled her determination to advocate for change, both within educational institutions and in society at large.

### 1.1.8 Discovering the LGBTQ Community

Wai Wai's journey of self-discovery led her to the LGBTQ community, where she found a sense of belonging that had eluded her in mainstream society. This community, though marginalized, was vibrant and resilient, offering a space for individuals to express their identities freely. Through participation in community events and gatherings, Wai Wai began to understand the power of collective action and the importance of visibility in the fight for rights.

### 1.1.9 The Impact of Religion

Religion plays a significant role in shaping societal attitudes towards LGBTQ individuals in Myanmar. Many religious teachings promote conservative views on sexuality and gender, contributing to the stigma surrounding LGBTQ identities. However, Wai Wai also encountered progressive interpretations of faith that embraced inclusivity and acceptance. This duality highlighted the complexities of navigating one's identity in a society where religious beliefs can both uplift and oppress.

In conclusion, growing up in a traditional society like Myanmar presents unique challenges for LGBTQ individuals. The interplay of culture, religion, and societal expectations creates a landscape fraught with difficulties, yet it also provides fertile ground for activism and change. Wai Wai Nu's journey exemplifies the resilience of those who dare to challenge the status quo in pursuit of equality and acceptance.

ERROR. thisXsection() returned an empty string with textbook depth = 3.

ERROR. thisXsection() returned an empty string with textbook depth = 3.

ERROR. thisXsection() returned an empty string with textbook depth = 3.

## The Influence of Burmese Culture

Burmese culture is a rich tapestry woven from various threads of history, religion, and social norms, all of which significantly shape the lives of its people, including the LGBTQ community. At the heart of this culture lies Buddhism, which permeates daily life, moral values, and societal expectations. Understanding the influence of Burmese culture is crucial in comprehending the challenges faced by LGBTQ individuals in Myanmar.

Buddhism, as the predominant religion in Myanmar, promotes values such as compassion, mindfulness, and non-attachment. However, these ideals often clash with traditional views on gender and sexuality. The teachings of Buddhism can be interpreted in various ways, leading to differing attitudes towards LGBTQ individuals. While some Buddhist philosophies emphasize compassion and acceptance, conservative interpretations frequently uphold heteronormative standards. This creates a complex environment where LGBTQ identities are often marginalized.

The traditional family structure in Myanmar plays a pivotal role in shaping societal attitudes towards LGBTQ individuals. Family honor and reputation are paramount, leading to immense pressure on individuals to conform to societal norms. Many LGBTQ individuals grow up in environments where their sexual orientation or gender identity is seen as a source of shame. This familial pressure can lead to internalized homophobia and a fear of rejection, which stifles the expression of one's true self.

Moreover, the concept of "*nats,*" or spirits, is integral to Burmese culture. Nats are believed to inhabit the natural world and are often associated with specific locations or events. Some LGBTQ individuals find solace in the belief that they may be connected to these spirits, which can provide a sense of identity and community. However, the intersection of nat worship and LGBTQ identity can be fraught with tension, as traditional beliefs may not fully embrace non-heteronormative expressions of love and identity.

A significant aspect of Burmese culture is the influence of colonial history, which has left a lasting impact on societal norms and legal frameworks. The British colonial era introduced laws that criminalized homosexuality, and these laws have persisted in various forms even after Myanmar gained independence. This colonial legacy has contributed to a culture of silence and stigma surrounding LGBTQ issues, making it difficult for individuals to advocate for their rights.

Despite these challenges, there are pockets of resistance and acceptance within Burmese culture. The emergence of the *"kathoey,"* or transgender women, in Thai culture has begun to influence perceptions in Myanmar. Although kathoey individuals often face discrimination, their visibility has sparked conversations about gender identity and fluidity. This growing awareness provides a glimmer of hope for LGBTQ individuals seeking acceptance in a society steeped in tradition.

Furthermore, the role of art and literature in Burmese culture cannot be overlooked. Artists and writers have begun to explore themes of love, identity, and gender, challenging traditional narratives. For instance, contemporary Burmese literature often features LGBTQ characters and stories, allowing for a broader representation of diverse identities. This artistic expression is vital in fostering understanding and empathy within the larger society.

In conclusion, the influence of Burmese culture on LGBTQ individuals is multifaceted, encompassing religious beliefs, family dynamics, colonial legacies, and emerging narratives in art and literature. While challenges remain, the evolving discourse surrounding LGBTQ rights and identities in Myanmar offers a pathway toward greater acceptance and understanding. By navigating the complexities of their cultural landscape, LGBTQ activists like Wai Wai Nu strive to create a more inclusive society, where love and identity can flourish without fear or stigma.

## Prejudices and Discrimination

In Myanmar, societal norms are deeply rooted in traditional values, which often leads to significant prejudices and discrimination against LGBTQ individuals. The cultural landscape is predominantly influenced by conservative interpretations of religion, particularly Buddhism, which can perpetuate negative stereotypes about sexual and gender minorities. This section explores the various dimensions of prejudice and discrimination that LGBTQ individuals face in Myanmar, drawing on theoretical frameworks and real-life examples.

### Cultural and Religious Influences

The intersection of culture and religion plays a crucial role in shaping societal attitudes towards LGBTQ individuals. In Myanmar, traditional beliefs often view homosexuality as a deviation from the norm, which fosters an environment of intolerance. The concept of *"moral integrity"* is often cited in opposition to LGBTQ rights, suggesting that non-heteronormative identities threaten the moral fabric of society. This perspective can be analyzed through the lens of *social identity theory*, which posits that individuals derive a sense of self from their group memberships, leading to in-group favoritism and out-group discrimination.

For instance, a study conducted by the Myanmar LGBTQ Network revealed that 65% of LGBTQ respondents reported experiencing discrimination in public spaces, with many citing religious gatherings as sites of hostility. This illustrates how cultural and religious narratives can create hostile environments for LGBTQ individuals, reinforcing their marginalization.

## Institutional Discrimination

Beyond cultural prejudices, institutional discrimination also plays a significant role in perpetuating inequalities. Laws that criminalize homosexuality, such as Section 377 of the Penal Code, not only reflect societal attitudes but also institutionalize discrimination. This legal framework creates barriers for LGBTQ individuals seeking justice and protection, as they are often reluctant to report violence or harassment due to fear of further victimization.

For example, in 2018, a young gay man was brutally attacked in Yangon. When he sought assistance from the police, he was met with ridicule and indifference, which discouraged him from pursuing legal action. This incident highlights the systemic nature of discrimination, where legal and institutional frameworks fail to protect vulnerable populations.

## Intersectionality and Discrimination

The concept of *intersectionality* is vital in understanding how different forms of discrimination intersect to create unique experiences for LGBTQ individuals. Many members of the LGBTQ community in Myanmar also belong to ethnic minorities, which compounds the challenges they face. For instance, LGBTQ individuals from the Rohingya community encounter not only homophobia but also ethnic discrimination, leading to a double marginalization.

A case study of a Rohingya transgender woman illustrates this intersectionality. She faced rejection from her community due to her gender identity and was further marginalized by the broader society, which viewed her as an outsider. This scenario exemplifies how intersectional identities can exacerbate experiences of prejudice and discrimination, creating a complex web of challenges that require nuanced approaches to advocacy and support.

## Psychological Impact of Discrimination

The psychological ramifications of prejudice and discrimination are profound. LGBTQ individuals in Myanmar often experience internalized homophobia, leading to mental health issues such as anxiety and depression. The stigma associated with being LGBTQ can result in feelings of shame and isolation, which are compounded by societal rejection.

Research indicates that LGBTQ individuals who face discrimination are at a higher risk of mental health disorders. A survey by the Myanmar Mental Health Association found that 72% of LGBTQ respondents reported symptoms of anxiety, with many attributing their distress to societal rejection and discrimination. This highlights the urgent need for mental health support tailored to the unique experiences of LGBTQ individuals.

## The Role of Activism in Challenging Prejudices

Despite the pervasive discrimination, activism plays a crucial role in challenging prejudices and advocating for LGBTQ rights. Organizations such as the Myanmar LGBTQ Network and other grassroots movements have emerged to raise awareness and promote acceptance. These organizations work to educate the public about LGBTQ issues, challenge discriminatory laws, and provide support to those affected by prejudice.

For example, the annual Pride Parade in Yangon has become a symbol of resistance and visibility for the LGBTQ community. It serves not only as a celebration of identity but also as a platform for raising awareness about the discrimination faced by LGBTQ individuals in Myanmar. Such events foster solidarity and empower individuals to embrace their identities, challenging the status quo of prejudice.

## Conclusion

Prejudices and discrimination against LGBTQ individuals in Myanmar are deeply entrenched in cultural, religious, and institutional frameworks. Understanding these dynamics through the lenses of social identity theory, intersectionality, and the psychological impact of discrimination is essential for developing effective advocacy strategies. As activism continues to grow, there is hope for a more inclusive society that values diversity and promotes equality for all individuals, regardless of their sexual orientation or gender identity.

## A Fearful Secret

Growing up in a traditional society like Myanmar, where deeply rooted cultural norms often dictate personal identity and expression, Wai Wai Nu faced a profound internal struggle. The societal expectations surrounding gender and sexuality created an environment that was both stifling and perilous for those who dared to deviate from the norm. This section delves into the complexities of living with a secret that could potentially jeopardize not only personal safety but also familial bonds and social standing.

From an early age, Wai Wai understood the unspoken rules of her community. The pervasive beliefs surrounding femininity and masculinity were not merely suggestions; they were laws of survival. As she navigated her childhood in Yangon, the weight of these expectations pressed down on her, creating a chasm between her authentic self and the persona she projected to the world. The fear of being discovered—of having her truth laid bare—loomed large, casting a shadow over her formative years.

The concept of *internalized homophobia* is crucial in understanding Wai Wai's experience. Internalized homophobia refers to the internalization of societal stigma, leading individuals to feel shame or self-hatred regarding their sexual orientation. This psychological phenomenon can manifest in various ways, including anxiety, depression, and a reluctance to embrace one's identity. For Wai Wai, the fear of rejection from her family and community was palpable, creating a cycle of secrecy and self-denial.

$$\text{Internalized Homophobia} \rightarrow \text{Anxiety} + \text{Depression} + \text{Secrecy} \qquad (1)$$

The need for secrecy was compounded by the harsh realities of discrimination faced by LGBTQ individuals in Myanmar. The criminalization of homosexuality, coupled with societal prejudice, meant that revealing her identity could lead to dire consequences. Stories of individuals who had faced violence, ostracism, or even imprisonment for being true to themselves circulated within the LGBTQ community, reinforcing the notion that safety lay in silence.

Wai Wai's fears were not unfounded; they were echoes of a systemic issue that plagued many in her community. The cultural narrative surrounding LGBTQ identities was often steeped in misunderstanding and hostility, leaving little room for compassion or acceptance. In a society where familial honor and reputation held immense value, the stakes of her secret were unbearably high.

The psychological toll of maintaining such a secret was significant. Wai Wai grappled with feelings of isolation and despair, often questioning her worth and place in a world that seemed to reject her very existence. The internal conflict she experienced was a reflection of the broader societal conflict between tradition and modernity—a clash that left many like her caught in the crossfire.

$$\text{Isolation} + \text{Despair} \rightarrow \text{Questioning Self-Worth} \qquad (2)$$

Despite the overwhelming fear, there were glimmers of hope. Wai Wai found solace in the company of a few close friends who shared similar experiences. These relationships became a lifeline, providing a safe space for her to express her true self, albeit in hushed tones. They navigated the treacherous waters of their identities together, often sharing stories of their struggles and dreams of a more accepting future.

The act of sharing her secret, even with a select few, began to alleviate some of the burdens she carried. It was a small rebellion against the silence that had suffocated her for so long. This camaraderie among friends not only fostered a sense of belonging but also ignited the embers of activism within her. She began to realize that her fear could be transformed into strength—a strength that could be harnessed to challenge the very norms that had kept her silent.

In conclusion, Wai Wai Nu's experience of living with a fearful secret highlights the profound impact of societal expectations on individual identity. The fear of rejection and violence, fueled by internalized homophobia and cultural stigma, created a complex web of secrecy that many LGBTQ individuals navigate daily. However, through the support of friends and the gradual acceptance of her identity, Wai Wai began to understand that her truth was not just a secret to be hidden but a powerful narrative waiting to be shared. This realization would ultimately serve as a catalyst for her journey into activism, where she would advocate for a world where no one would have to live in fear of their identity.

## The Beginnings of Activism

Wai Wai Nu's journey into activism began in the crucible of her formative years, shaped by the harsh realities of a traditional society that often stifled individuality. In Myanmar, where cultural norms and expectations are deeply entrenched, the act of standing up for one's rights—especially for LGBTQ individuals—was not just a personal struggle; it was a radical act of defiance.

The initial spark of activism ignited when Wai Wai began to understand the extent of discrimination faced by the LGBTQ community in her country. Growing up in Yangon, she was acutely aware of the societal pressures that dictated conformity. The pervasive attitudes towards gender and sexual identity were not merely personal opinions but were woven into the very fabric of Burmese culture.

This cultural backdrop often perpetuated harmful stereotypes and fostered an environment where fear and silence dominated the LGBTQ narrative.

$$Activism = Awareness + Courage + Community \quad\quad (3)$$

To Wai Wai, awareness was the first step. She began to educate herself about the struggles of LGBTQ individuals, both within her community and globally. This education was not limited to reading books or attending lectures; it involved engaging in conversations with peers and seeking out stories of resilience and resistance. She found inspiration in the works of activists from other countries, whose struggles mirrored her own yet showcased the power of visibility and solidarity.

However, this newfound awareness came with its own set of challenges. The fear of ostracization loomed large. Many individuals in her community viewed LGBTQ identities through a lens of prejudice, often equating them with moral decay. This societal stigma created a dichotomy in Wai Wai's life—on one hand, she yearned for authenticity and connection, while on the other, she faced the daunting prospect of rejection from family and friends.

It was during this tumultuous period that Wai Wai discovered the importance of finding support in unexpected places. She began to connect with other LGBTQ individuals, both online and offline. These connections became lifelines; they provided her with a sense of belonging and understanding that was often absent in her immediate environment. The realization that she was not alone in her struggles galvanized her resolve to fight for change.

The act of navigating school and society presented its own set of hurdles. Educational institutions often mirrored the prejudices of the larger society, with bullying and discrimination rampant against those who dared to be different. Wai Wai became acutely aware of the need for safe spaces where LGBTQ youth could express themselves without fear of retribution. This realization sparked her first efforts in activism, as she began organizing small gatherings with like-minded peers to discuss their experiences and strategize ways to foster acceptance within their schools.

The impact of religion in Myanmar cannot be understated; it often dictated social norms and influenced public opinion on LGBTQ issues. Wai Wai found herself grappling with the teachings of Buddhism, which, while promoting compassion, often fell short in its acceptance of sexual diversity. This conflict led her to question the narratives she had been taught and to seek interpretations that embraced love and acceptance rather than exclusion.

As she delved deeper into activism, Wai Wai started to embrace her identity more fully. She began to accept and embrace her differences, recognizing that her unique experiences could serve as a powerful tool for change. The struggle for self-acceptance was ongoing, but each step she took towards authenticity fortified her resolve to advocate for others facing similar challenges.

In her early attempts at activism, Wai Wai faced numerous obstacles, including threats and the risk of public scrutiny. However, these challenges only fueled her determination to create a more inclusive society. She began to speak out against discrimination, leveraging social media platforms to raise awareness and connect with a broader audience. The power of visibility became a central theme in her activism, as she understood that sharing her story could inspire others to do the same.

Through her grassroots efforts, Wai Wai initiated community events aimed at fostering dialogue and understanding between LGBTQ individuals and the broader society. These events not only provided a platform for marginalized voices but also served to educate allies and challenge prevailing prejudices. The response was mixed; while many embraced the opportunity for connection and learning, others reacted with hostility, highlighting the deep-seated biases that persisted in Myanmar.

In summary, the beginnings of Wai Wai Nu's activism were marked by a profound journey of self-discovery, education, and community building. Her experiences underscored the importance of visibility, support, and resilience in the face of adversity. As she navigated the complexities of her identity and the societal expectations placed upon her, Wai Wai laid the groundwork for a movement that would seek to challenge discrimination and promote acceptance for all LGBTQ individuals in Myanmar.

## Finding Support in Unexpected Places

In the journey of self-discovery and activism, one often finds that support can emerge from the most unexpected corners of life. For Wai Wai Nu, navigating the complexities of her identity as an LGBTQ individual in Myanmar was fraught with challenges, yet it was also marked by moments of serendipitous connection and solidarity. This section explores how these unexpected sources of support played a crucial role in her development as an activist and a leader.

### The Role of Family

While many LGBTQ individuals face rejection from their families, Wai Wai's experience was nuanced. Her family's traditional values often clashed with her emerging identity, yet there were glimmers of acceptance that provided her with a foundation of support. For instance, her mother, despite her initial reservations, began to understand the struggles faced by her daughter through conversations that highlighted the universal themes of love and acceptance. This familial support, albeit complicated, became a source of strength for Wai Wai, allowing her to embrace her identity with greater confidence.

## Friendships as Safe Havens

Friendships often serve as lifelines in times of distress. Wai Wai found solace in a close-knit group of friends who shared similar experiences. These relationships were characterized by mutual understanding and empathy, creating a safe space where she could express her fears and aspirations without judgment. The importance of these friendships cannot be overstated; they provided emotional support and practical advice, reinforcing the notion that community can be found in the most unlikely of places.

## Unexpected Allies in Academia

Wai Wai's academic journey also introduced her to unexpected allies. Professors and classmates who were sympathetic to her plight became instrumental in her quest for self-acceptance and activism. For example, during a university seminar on human rights, a professor encouraged open discussions about LGBTQ issues, creating an environment where students could explore and challenge societal norms. This academic support not only validated Wai Wai's experiences but also empowered her to articulate her thoughts on LGBTQ rights more effectively.

## Engaging with Local NGOs

In her quest for support, Wai Wai discovered local non-governmental organizations (NGOs) that focused on human rights and social justice. These organizations often operated in the shadows of Myanmar's political landscape, yet they provided critical resources and networks for LGBTQ individuals. By engaging with these NGOs, Wai Wai found mentorship and guidance from seasoned activists who had navigated similar challenges. This collaboration was pivotal in helping her understand the broader context of LGBTQ rights within Myanmar and the strategies necessary for effective advocacy.

## The Power of Online Communities

In an increasingly digital world, online communities have emerged as vital sources of support for marginalized individuals. Wai Wai leveraged social media platforms to connect with LGBTQ activists both locally and internationally. These online interactions provided her with a sense of belonging and the realization that her struggles were shared by many. The exchange of stories and resources through these platforms fostered a sense of solidarity that transcended geographical boundaries, illustrating the power of technology in bridging gaps between individuals facing similar challenges.

## Cultural and Artistic Expression

Unexpected support also manifested through cultural and artistic expression. The arts have long been a vehicle for social change, and Wai Wai found inspiration in the works of LGBTQ artists and writers who challenged societal norms. Local theater productions that addressed LGBTQ themes became a source of empowerment, allowing her to see her experiences reflected in the narratives of others. This cultural engagement not only validated her identity but also motivated her to contribute her voice to the ongoing discourse surrounding LGBTQ rights in Myanmar.

## Spiritual Communities

Another surprising source of support came from within spiritual communities. While traditional religious beliefs often perpetuate discrimination against LGBTQ individuals, some progressive religious groups in Myanmar began to advocate for inclusion and acceptance. Wai Wai's interactions with these groups revealed the potential for faith-based support in the fight for LGBTQ rights. By participating in inclusive religious gatherings, she found a space where spirituality and activism coalesced, allowing her to reconcile her identity with her beliefs.

## Conclusion

Ultimately, the journey of finding support in unexpected places underscores a fundamental truth: community is often built on shared experiences and mutual understanding. For Wai Wai Nu, the diverse sources of support she encountered—family, friends, academia, NGOs, online networks, the arts, and spiritual communities—were instrumental in shaping her identity and fueling her activism. These connections not only provided her with the strength to confront societal prejudices but also illuminated the path toward a more inclusive future for LGBTQ individuals in Myanmar.

As she reflects on her journey, Wai Wai recognizes that the power of unexpected support lies not only in its ability to uplift individuals but also in its potential to foster a collective movement for change. By embracing the connections formed through shared experiences, activists like Wai Wai can continue to challenge societal norms and advocate for a world where love and acceptance prevail over prejudice and discrimination.

## Navigating School and Society

In Myanmar, navigating the complexities of school and society as a member of the LGBTQ community presents a unique set of challenges. The traditional norms and values that permeate Burmese culture often create an environment where LGBTQ individuals face significant discrimination and stigma. This section explores the multifaceted experiences of LGBTQ youth in educational settings and broader societal contexts, highlighting the intersection of cultural expectations, peer dynamics, and the quest for identity.

### The Educational Landscape

Schools in Myanmar are not merely places of learning; they are microcosms of society where cultural norms are reinforced and perpetuated. The rigid gender roles and expectations prevalent in the broader community often manifest in school environments, making it difficult for LGBTQ students to express their identities openly.

$$C = \frac{S}{R} \tag{4}$$

where $C$ represents cultural acceptance, $S$ signifies support from peers and educators, and $R$ denotes resistance from societal norms. A low value of $C$ indicates a challenging environment for LGBTQ students, where the support system is weak, and resistance is strong.

### Peer Dynamics

Peer relationships play a crucial role in shaping the school experience for LGBTQ youth. The fear of bullying and ostracism often leads students to conceal their identities. Research shows that LGBTQ students are more likely to experience harassment in schools compared to their heterosexual peers. This harassment can take various forms, including verbal abuse, physical violence, and social exclusion.

A study conducted by the *Myanmar Youth Coalition* revealed that approximately 60% of LGBTQ students reported experiencing bullying, which significantly impacts their mental health and academic performance. The constant pressure to conform to heteronormative standards often leads to feelings of isolation and anxiety.

$$M = \frac{B + E}{A} \tag{5}$$

In this equation, $M$ represents mental health outcomes, $B$ is the level of bullying experienced, $E$ signifies external support received, and $A$ denotes academic achievement. Higher levels of bullying ($B$) without adequate support ($E$) correlate with poorer mental health outcomes ($M$) and lower academic performance ($A$).

## Cultural Expectations and Identity Formation

The pressure to conform to traditional gender roles complicates the journey of self-acceptance for LGBTQ youth. In a culture where familial honor and societal reputation are paramount, coming out can be fraught with fear and anxiety. Many LGBTQ individuals navigate a delicate balance between their authentic selves and the expectations imposed by their families and communities.

This struggle is often exacerbated by the influence of religion, which can serve as both a source of comfort and a tool of oppression. For instance, conservative interpretations of Buddhism in Myanmar often promote traditional family structures, leaving little room for LGBTQ identities. Consequently, many students grapple with internalized homophobia, fearing rejection from their families and communities.

## Finding Allies and Support

Despite these challenges, LGBTQ students often find allies in unexpected places. Supportive teachers, friends, and community organizations can provide crucial resources and safe spaces for self-expression. Initiatives such as LGBTQ clubs and awareness programs in schools can foster a sense of belonging and community among students.

For example, the *Rainbow Youth Network* in Yangon has been instrumental in creating safe spaces for LGBTQ youth. Through workshops and peer support groups, they empower students to embrace their identities and advocate for their rights within the school system.

## The Role of Education in Changing Perspectives

Education plays a pivotal role in challenging stereotypes and fostering acceptance. LGBTQ-inclusive curricula can help dismantle prejudices and promote understanding among students. By integrating discussions about gender and sexual diversity into educational programs, schools can cultivate a more inclusive environment.

$$A = E + C \tag{6}$$

In this equation, $A$ represents acceptance, $E$ signifies education, and $C$ denotes community engagement. A comprehensive approach that combines education with community involvement can lead to greater acceptance ($A$) of LGBTQ individuals in schools and society at large.

## Conclusion

Navigating school and society as an LGBTQ individual in Myanmar is a complex journey marked by challenges and opportunities. While cultural expectations and peer dynamics can create barriers to self-acceptance and expression, the resilience and activism of LGBTQ youth demonstrate the potential for change. By fostering supportive environments and promoting inclusive education, society can work towards dismantling the stigma surrounding LGBTQ identities, paving the way for a more inclusive future.

Through the stories of those who have navigated this path, we can better understand the importance of allyship, education, and advocacy in creating a society where all individuals, regardless of their sexual orientation or gender identity, can thrive.

## Discovering the LGBTQ Community

Wai Wai Nu's journey into the LGBTQ community was not merely a process of self-discovery; it was a profound awakening to a world that existed in the shadows of Myanmar's traditional society. The realization of belonging to a community that shared her struggles and aspirations was both liberating and daunting.

In Myanmar, where cultural norms are steeped in conservatism, the LGBTQ community often operated clandestinely, forming tight-knit networks that provided support and solace. The first encounter with this community came during her teenage years, when Wai Wai stumbled upon a small gathering of individuals who, like her, were navigating the complexities of their identities in a society that largely rejected them.

The importance of community in LGBTQ activism cannot be overstated. According to queer theory, community can serve as a site of resistance against dominant cultural narratives that marginalize LGBTQ identities. Judith Butler, a prominent figure in queer theory, argues that identities are not fixed but are instead performed through social interactions. This notion resonated with Wai Wai as she began to understand that her identity was not just a personal journey but part of a collective experience.

$$I = P + S \qquad (7)$$

Where $I$ represents identity, $P$ is personal experience, and $S$ is social interaction. This equation illustrates how identity is shaped by both personal narratives and community interactions.

Wai Wai's initial involvement with the LGBTQ community was fraught with challenges. Prejudices and discrimination were pervasive, and the fear of exposure loomed large. Many individuals she met had faced severe repercussions for their identities—ranging from familial rejection to violence. Yet, it was within this context of shared adversity that bonds were forged.

The gatherings often took place in private homes or secluded venues, away from the prying eyes of society. Here, they shared stories, laughter, and tears, creating a safe space where they could express their true selves without fear of judgment. This underground network was crucial for fostering resilience and solidarity among its members.

Wai Wai also discovered the power of art and expression within the community. Many LGBTQ individuals used poetry, dance, and visual arts as forms of resistance and self-affirmation. For instance, local artists began to create works that challenged societal norms and celebrated queer identities. This artistic expression served not only as a means of coping but also as a powerful tool for advocacy.

Furthermore, the community began to organize informal support groups, where members could discuss their experiences and strategize on how to navigate the societal landscape. These meetings were often filled with a mix of vulnerability and strength, as individuals shared their fears while also encouraging one another to embrace their identities.

$$R = C + S \qquad (8)$$

Where $R$ represents resilience, $C$ is community support, and $S$ is shared experiences. This equation highlights how resilience in the LGBTQ community is cultivated through the strength derived from communal ties and shared narratives.

As Wai Wai became more involved, she realized the importance of visibility. The act of being seen and heard was an essential step toward challenging the stigma surrounding LGBTQ identities in Myanmar. Visibility, as discussed in the works of Michel Foucault, is a form of power that can disrupt the status quo. By sharing their stories publicly, LGBTQ individuals could reclaim their narratives and assert their existence in a society that often rendered them invisible.

The discovery of the LGBTQ community also opened Wai Wai's eyes to the intersectionality of identities. She learned that the struggles faced by LGBTQ individuals were compounded by other factors such as ethnicity, class, and religion. This realization deepened her understanding of the complexities of identity and the need for an inclusive movement that addressed the diverse experiences within the community.

In essence, discovering the LGBTQ community was a transformative experience for Wai Wai Nu. It provided her with the support, understanding, and courage to embrace her identity fully. The connections she formed within this community would lay the groundwork for her future activism, as she recognized that fighting for LGBTQ rights in Myanmar was not just about her own journey but about advocating for the rights and dignity of all marginalized individuals.

Through the lens of her experiences, Wai Wai began to envision a future where acceptance and love could flourish, and where the LGBTQ community could stand proudly in the light, no longer hidden in the shadows.

## The Impact of Religion

Religion plays a significant role in shaping societal norms and values, especially in conservative societies like Myanmar. The predominant religion in Myanmar is Buddhism, which deeply influences the cultural landscape and the perception of LGBTQ identities. This section explores the complexities of religious beliefs in relation to LGBTQ rights, the challenges faced by LGBTQ individuals, and the potential for change within religious contexts.

### Buddhism and Its Teachings

Buddhism, as practiced in Myanmar, emphasizes the concepts of morality, compassion, and non-harm (ahimsa). However, interpretations of these teachings can vary widely. Traditional Buddhist teachings do not explicitly condemn homosexuality; instead, they focus on the intention behind actions. The Pali Canon, the primary scripture of Theravada Buddhism, does not contain direct references to same-sex relationships. Yet, cultural interpretations often lead to stigmatization of LGBTQ individuals.

## Cultural Interpretations and Prejudices

Despite the absence of explicit prohibitions, many Buddhists in Myanmar interpret their faith in a way that aligns with heteronormative values. This has resulted in a societal framework where LGBTQ identities are often viewed as deviant or immoral. The societal pressure to conform to traditional gender roles and heterosexual relationships can lead to internalized homophobia among LGBTQ individuals, creating a cycle of shame and fear.

## Religious Institutions and LGBTQ Rights

Religious institutions in Myanmar often play a pivotal role in community life, and their stance on LGBTQ issues can significantly influence public opinion. Many religious leaders promote conservative views, reinforcing the belief that LGBTQ identities are incompatible with Buddhist values. This has led to resistance against LGBTQ rights advocacy, as activists face pushback not only from the government but also from religious groups.

For instance, during community gatherings or sermons, religious leaders may emphasize the importance of traditional family structures, often using rhetoric that marginalizes LGBTQ individuals. This public discourse can perpetuate discrimination and violence against the LGBTQ community, making it difficult for individuals to live authentically.

## The Role of Faith in LGBTQ Activism

Despite the challenges posed by religious beliefs, there are emerging voices within the Buddhist community advocating for LGBTQ acceptance. Some progressive monks and laypeople are beginning to reinterpret Buddhist teachings in a way that embraces diversity and promotes compassion. This shift indicates a potential for dialogue between LGBTQ activists and religious leaders, fostering a more inclusive understanding of faith.

For example, initiatives such as LGBTQ-inclusive meditation retreats and workshops led by supportive monks aim to create safe spaces for LGBTQ individuals within the religious context. These efforts highlight the possibility of reconciling faith and identity, allowing individuals to embrace both their spirituality and their sexual orientation.

## Intersectionality of Religion and LGBTQ Identity

The impact of religion on LGBTQ individuals is further complicated by the intersectionality of various identities, including ethnicity, gender, and socioeconomic status. For instance, individuals from ethnic minority groups may face compounded discrimination, as their sexual orientation is scrutinized not only through the lens of religion but also through ethnic prejudices. This intersectional approach is crucial for understanding the diverse experiences of LGBTQ individuals in Myanmar.

Research has shown that LGBTQ individuals from marginalized ethnic backgrounds often encounter unique challenges, such as limited access to resources and support networks. This highlights the need for an inclusive framework that addresses the specific needs of these individuals while considering the influence of religion.

## Towards a More Inclusive Future

As Myanmar continues to evolve, the role of religion in shaping LGBTQ rights will remain a critical area of focus. Engaging religious leaders in conversations about inclusivity and compassion can pave the way for greater acceptance. By fostering dialogue and understanding, it is possible to challenge the prevailing narratives that perpetuate discrimination.

In conclusion, while religion poses significant challenges for LGBTQ individuals in Myanmar, it also holds the potential for transformation. By embracing the core teachings of compassion and non-harm, there is an opportunity to create a more inclusive society that respects and honors the identities of all individuals, regardless of their sexual orientation or gender identity. The path forward requires courage, empathy, and a commitment to challenging the status quo, ultimately leading to a more harmonious coexistence of faith and LGBTQ identities.

# Confronting Gender and Sexual Identity

## Accepting and Embracing Differences

In the journey toward self-acceptance, the process of recognizing and embracing one's differences is both profound and transformative. For many individuals, particularly those within the LGBTQ community, this journey is often fraught with challenges stemming from societal norms and cultural expectations. Accepting and embracing differences involves understanding the complexities of identity, which can encompass sexual orientation, gender identity, and cultural background.

## Theoretical Framework

The concept of self-acceptance is rooted in various psychological theories. One prominent theory is Carl Rogers' Humanistic Psychology, which emphasizes the importance of self-concept and unconditional positive regard. According to Rogers, individuals must accept themselves fully to achieve personal growth and self-actualization. This theory is particularly relevant for LGBTQ individuals who may struggle with internalized homophobia or transphobia, often stemming from societal rejection.

Another relevant framework is the Social Identity Theory proposed by Henri Tajfel and John Turner. This theory posits that individuals derive part of their identity from the social groups to which they belong. For LGBTQ individuals, embracing their sexual or gender identity can lead to a stronger sense of belonging and community, counteracting feelings of isolation often perpetuated by societal prejudice.

## Challenges in Acceptance

Despite the theoretical underpinnings that support self-acceptance, various challenges can impede this process. One significant barrier is the internalized stigma that many LGBTQ individuals face. This stigma can manifest as feelings of shame, guilt, or self-hatred, often exacerbated by negative societal messages. For instance, individuals may grapple with the fear of rejection from family and friends, leading to a reluctance to embrace their true selves.

Furthermore, cultural expectations can create additional pressure. In traditional societies, where conformity to heteronormative standards is often enforced, deviating from these norms can result in ostracism. This cultural context can lead to a profound internal struggle as individuals weigh their desire for authenticity against the potential repercussions of embracing their differences.

## Examples of Embracing Differences

Despite these challenges, many LGBTQ individuals have found ways to accept and embrace their differences, often serving as powerful examples for others. One notable figure is Wai Wai Nu, who, despite facing significant adversity, has become a beacon of hope and inspiration for the LGBTQ community in Myanmar. Her journey of self-acceptance involved confronting her own fears and societal prejudices, ultimately leading her to embrace her identity fully.

Wai Wai's story exemplifies the power of community support in the acceptance process. By connecting with other LGBTQ individuals, she found solace and strength in shared experiences. This sense of belonging not only helped her accept her differences but also motivated her to advocate for others facing similar struggles.

Another example is the global phenomenon of Pride events. These celebrations serve as a testament to the power of embracing differences, showcasing the diversity within the LGBTQ community. Participants often describe a sense of liberation and joy when they come together to celebrate their identities openly. Such events challenge societal norms and foster a culture of acceptance, encouraging individuals to embrace their uniqueness.

## The Importance of Embracing Differences

Embracing differences is not just a personal journey; it has broader societal implications. When individuals accept and celebrate their identities, they contribute to a more inclusive and diverse society. This acceptance can lead to increased visibility for marginalized communities, fostering understanding and empathy among those outside the LGBTQ community.

Moreover, embracing differences can catalyze social change. As individuals share their stories and experiences, they challenge stereotypes and prejudices, paving the way for greater acceptance and legal protections. This ripple effect can inspire others to embark on their own journeys of self-acceptance, creating a more supportive environment for all.

## Conclusion

In conclusion, accepting and embracing differences is a critical component of the LGBTQ experience. Through theoretical frameworks, personal examples, and the acknowledgment of societal challenges, it becomes clear that this journey is both complex and essential. By fostering a culture of acceptance, individuals can not only transform their own lives but also contribute to a more inclusive society that values diversity in all its forms. The path toward self-acceptance is not always easy, but it is a vital step in the fight for equality and recognition within a world that often seeks to suppress differences.

## The Struggle for Self-Acceptance

The journey toward self-acceptance is often fraught with challenges, particularly for individuals navigating their identities within a traditional society. For Wai Wai Nu, growing up in Myanmar—a country steeped in conservative values and cultural expectations—this struggle was compounded by societal prejudices against LGBTQ individuals. The process of self-acceptance is not merely an internal battle; it is deeply influenced by external factors, including family dynamics, cultural norms, and the pervasive stigma surrounding LGBTQ identities.

### Understanding Self-Acceptance

Self-acceptance refers to the recognition and embrace of one's identity, feelings, and experiences without judgment. According to *Tajfel's Social Identity Theory*, individuals derive a sense of self from their group memberships, which can significantly affect their self-esteem and overall well-being. In societies where LGBTQ identities are marginalized, individuals may experience a dissonance between their self-concept and societal expectations, leading to internalized homophobia and self-rejection.

### The Role of Cultural Expectations

In Myanmar, traditional beliefs often dictate rigid gender roles and expectations regarding sexuality. This cultural backdrop creates a landscape where deviations from the norm are met with hostility and discrimination. Wai Wai Nu found herself grappling with the weight of these expectations. The pressure to conform to societal norms can lead to feelings of inadequacy and self-doubt. As she navigated her teenage years, the clash between her emerging identity and the cultural narrative surrounding LGBTQ individuals became increasingly apparent.

### The Impact of Family Dynamics

Family plays a crucial role in shaping one's self-acceptance journey. In many cases, the fear of rejection from family members can lead to a reluctance to embrace one's true self. Wai Wai Nu's experience was no exception. Coming from a traditional family, the prospect of revealing her sexual orientation was daunting. The potential for familial rejection created a barrier to her self-acceptance, forcing her to conceal her identity and live in fear of discovery.

## Internalized Homophobia

Internalized homophobia is a significant barrier to self-acceptance for many LGBTQ individuals. It occurs when individuals internalize society's negative attitudes towards homosexuality, leading to self-hatred and a rejection of their identity. For Wai Wai Nu, confronting internalized homophobia was a critical step in her journey. She struggled with feelings of shame and guilt, often questioning her worth and place in a society that deemed her identity as deviant.

## Finding Support and Community

Despite the challenges, the journey toward self-acceptance can be facilitated by finding supportive communities. Wai Wai Nu discovered that connecting with other LGBTQ individuals provided her with a sense of belonging and validation. Support groups and LGBTQ organizations serve as safe havens where individuals can share their experiences and challenges. This sense of community is vital for fostering self-acceptance, as it reinforces the idea that one is not alone in their struggles.

## The Role of Activism in Self-Acceptance

Engaging in activism can also play a transformative role in the journey toward self-acceptance. For Wai Wai Nu, becoming an advocate for LGBTQ rights allowed her to reclaim her narrative and challenge societal prejudices. Activism empowered her to embrace her identity and advocate for others facing similar struggles. The act of standing up for oneself and others can be a powerful catalyst for self-acceptance, as it fosters resilience and a sense of purpose.

## Conclusion

The struggle for self-acceptance is a multifaceted journey that encompasses personal, cultural, and societal dimensions. For Wai Wai Nu, navigating the complexities of her identity within a traditional society was an arduous process marked by fear, shame, and ultimately, empowerment. By confronting internalized homophobia, seeking support, and engaging in activism, she began to forge a path toward self-acceptance. This journey not only transformed her understanding of herself but also laid the groundwork for her future work as a fierce advocate for LGBTQ rights in Myanmar. The interplay of personal and societal factors underscores the importance of creating inclusive spaces where individuals can embrace their identities without fear of judgment or discrimination.

## Coming Out to Family and Friends

Coming out is often described as a pivotal moment in the lives of LGBTQ individuals, representing a journey toward authenticity and self-acceptance. For Wai Wai Nu, the process of revealing her sexual orientation to family and friends was fraught with anxiety, cultural implications, and the weight of societal expectations. This section explores the complexities of coming out in a traditional society like Myanmar, examining the challenges faced, the emotional toll, and the eventual liberation that can accompany such a profound revelation.

## Understanding the Coming Out Process

The coming out process is multifaceted, encompassing not only the disclosure of one's sexual orientation but also the internal struggle of self-acceptance. According to the *Cass Model of Sexual Identity Formation*, coming out is part of a broader developmental process that includes stages such as identity confusion, identity comparison, identity tolerance, identity acceptance, identity pride, and ultimately, identity synthesis [?]. For Wai Wai, each stage was marked by moments of doubt and clarity, as she navigated her feelings in a society that often viewed her identity as taboo.

## Cultural Context and Familial Expectations

In Myanmar, where traditional values dominate, the expectations placed on individuals regarding marriage, gender roles, and sexual orientation can be overwhelming. The pressure to conform to societal norms often leads LGBTQ individuals to suppress their identities. Wai Wai felt this pressure acutely as she grappled with her family's expectations for her future. The fear of disappointing her parents, who held conservative views, created a barrier that made coming out seem daunting.

Research indicates that familial acceptance plays a crucial role in the mental health and well-being of LGBTQ individuals [?]. The potential for rejection loomed large in Wai Wai's mind, leading to a profound sense of isolation. She often questioned whether her family would be able to understand or accept her truth, which compounded her anxiety.

## The Moment of Truth

The day Wai Wai chose to come out to her family was marked by a mixture of trepidation and resolve. She had spent countless nights rehearsing the conversation in her mind, weighing her words carefully. The act of coming out is not merely a verbal declaration; it is a moment filled with vulnerability and courage. As she sat across from her family, she felt her heart race, each beat echoing the uncertainty of their reaction.

Wai Wai's decision to come out was influenced by her growing involvement in the LGBTQ community, where she found solidarity and support. This newfound sense of belonging provided her with the strength to confront her fears. She began the conversation by expressing her love for her family, emphasizing that her identity did not diminish her commitment to them.

## Reactions and Consequences

The reactions of family members can vary widely, ranging from acceptance to rejection. In Wai Wai's case, her mother's initial response was one of shock and confusion, while her father struggled to reconcile his beliefs with his daughter's truth. The emotional fallout was palpable, as tears were shed and silence filled the room.

This moment highlights the psychological impact of coming out, as described by *Minority Stress Theory*. The theory posits that LGBTQ individuals often face unique stressors that can lead to mental health issues, including anxiety and depression [?]. The fear of rejection and the struggle for acceptance can create a significant emotional burden, as seen in Wai Wai's experience.

## Finding Support in Friendship

While the response from her family was mixed, Wai Wai found solace in her friendships. Friends who were part of the LGBTQ community provided her with the understanding and empathy that she craved. This underscores the importance of chosen families, which often become crucial support systems for LGBTQ individuals facing rejection from biological families [?].

Wai Wai's friends celebrated her bravery and offered encouragement, reminding her that her identity was valid and deserving of love. Their acceptance helped her navigate the tumultuous waters of familial rejection, reinforcing her belief in the importance of authenticity.

## The Journey Toward Acceptance

Over time, the initial shock of Wai Wai's revelation began to dissipate. Her family slowly started to engage in conversations about her identity, seeking to understand her experiences. This gradual acceptance illustrates the potential for growth and change within families, as they confront their biases and strive for understanding.

The journey of coming out does not end with a single conversation. It is an ongoing process that requires patience, education, and open dialogue. For Wai Wai, sharing resources about LGBTQ issues and fostering conversations about acceptance played a critical role in bridging the gap between her identity and her family's understanding.

## Conclusion: The Power of Authenticity

Ultimately, coming out to family and friends was a transformative experience for Wai Wai Nu. It marked a significant step toward embracing her identity and advocating for LGBTQ rights in Myanmar. While the journey was fraught with challenges, it also paved the way for deeper connections and a renewed sense of purpose.

Wai Wai's story exemplifies the resilience of LGBTQ individuals in the face of adversity and the profound impact that acceptance—both self-acceptance and acceptance from others—can have on one's mental health and overall well-being. As she continues her activism, Wai Wai stands as a testament to the power of living authentically, inspiring others to embrace their truths in a world that often seeks to silence them.

## Confronting Cultural Expectations

In Myanmar, cultural expectations surrounding gender and sexuality are deeply rooted in traditional beliefs and societal norms. These expectations often dictate how individuals should behave, whom they should love, and the roles they should fulfill within the family and community. For LGBTQ individuals like Wai Wai Nu, confronting these cultural expectations becomes a vital part of their journey toward self-acceptance and activism.

## The Weight of Tradition

The traditional Burmese society is influenced by a mix of Buddhist teachings and local customs, which often emphasize heteronormativity and gender binary roles. According to the theory of *social constructivism*, these norms are not inherent but are constructed through social interactions and cultural narratives. This creates a framework within which individuals are expected to navigate their identities. The pressure to conform can lead to internal conflict, as LGBTQ individuals struggle to reconcile their authentic selves with societal expectations.

## Family Expectations and Responsibilities

Family plays a pivotal role in shaping one's identity in Myanmar. For many, the expectation to marry and have children is paramount. As Wai Wai Nu navigated her coming out process, she faced the daunting task of confronting her family's expectations. The concept of *familial duty* in Burmese culture often supersedes individual desires, leading to feelings of guilt and shame for those who deviate from the norm.

For instance, when Wai Wai Nu came out to her family, she was met with resistance and disappointment. Her parents, like many others in similar situations, held onto the belief that their daughter's primary role was to marry a man and continue the family lineage. This pressure can create an environment where LGBTQ individuals feel compelled to hide their identities, leading to a phenomenon known as *internalized homophobia*.

## Navigating Community Expectations

Beyond family, the broader community also imposes expectations that can be stifling for LGBTQ individuals. In many instances, cultural narratives portray LGBTQ identities as deviant or immoral, leading to widespread discrimination and ostracization. The theory of *cultural hegemony*, as proposed by Antonio Gramsci, illustrates how dominant cultural norms maintain power over marginalized groups, perpetuating cycles of oppression.

Wai Wai Nu's experience in her community was marked by a constant negotiation between her identity and the expectations placed upon her. For example, attending community events often meant suppressing her true self to avoid backlash or ridicule. This duality can lead to feelings of isolation, as individuals feel they cannot fully participate in their communities without sacrificing their authenticity.

## Challenging Cultural Norms

Despite the challenges, confronting cultural expectations can also be a catalyst for change. Activists like Wai Wai Nu have begun to challenge these norms by advocating for greater acceptance and understanding within their communities. The theory of *intersectionality*, introduced by Kimberlé Crenshaw, highlights the interconnected nature of social categorizations and how they create overlapping systems of discrimination. By recognizing the intersection of gender, sexuality, and cultural identity, activists can address the unique challenges faced by LGBTQ individuals in Myanmar.

For instance, Wai Wai Nu organized workshops aimed at educating both LGBTQ individuals and the broader community about sexual orientation and gender identity. These initiatives not only provide a platform for discussion but also challenge the misconceptions that perpetuate discrimination. By fostering dialogue, activists can begin to dismantle the rigid cultural expectations that constrain individual expression.

## The Role of Media and Representation

Media representation also plays a crucial role in challenging cultural expectations. As LGBTQ narratives become more visible in local and international media, they provide alternative frameworks for understanding identity. The concept of *representation theory* posits that media portrayals shape societal perceptions and can influence cultural norms. Positive representations of LGBTQ individuals can help normalize diverse identities and challenge existing prejudices.

Wai Wai Nu's story, when shared through various media platforms, serves as a powerful testament to the resilience of LGBTQ individuals in Myanmar. By sharing her experiences, she not only confronts cultural expectations but also inspires others to embrace their identities and advocate for change.

## Conclusion

Confronting cultural expectations is a complex and often painful journey for LGBTQ individuals in Myanmar. The interplay of family, community, and media shapes the experiences of those who seek to live authentically. While the weight of tradition can be daunting, the efforts of activists like Wai Wai Nu highlight the potential for change. By challenging societal norms and fostering understanding, there is hope for a future where LGBTQ identities are embraced rather than marginalized. The struggle for acceptance is ongoing, but each act of defiance against cultural expectations paves the way for greater freedom and equality.

## Finding Love and Relationships

Finding love and forming relationships can be a transformative experience, particularly for individuals navigating their identities within a traditional society. For Wai Wai Nu, the journey towards love was intertwined with the struggle for self-acceptance and the desire for connection amidst societal pressures. This section explores the complexities of finding love as an LGBTQ individual in Myanmar, highlighting the challenges faced, the importance of community, and the joy that love can bring.

## The Search for Connection

In a society where traditional gender roles and expectations dominate, the search for love can feel daunting. The fear of rejection or discrimination often looms large. For Wai Wai, the initial encounters with love were fraught with uncertainty. The desire for intimacy was met with the reality of societal norms that dictated who one could love. This internal conflict is common among LGBTQ individuals, where the yearning for connection must be balanced against the fear of societal backlash.

$$\text{Fear of Rejection} = f(\text{Societal Norms, Cultural Expectations}) \qquad (9)$$

This equation illustrates that the fear of rejection is a function of societal norms and cultural expectations, which often dictate the parameters of acceptable relationships.

## Navigating Relationships

Wai Wai's experiences in navigating relationships reflect a broader struggle faced by many in the LGBTQ community. The process of coming out to potential partners is laden with anxiety. The question of whether to reveal one's identity can create significant tension. This tension is compounded by the reality that many LGBTQ individuals may have limited experiences with openly queer relationships, leading to feelings of isolation.

The importance of finding supportive partners cannot be overstated. A partner who understands and respects one's identity can provide a safe space for love to flourish. For Wai Wai, discovering a partner who shared similar experiences and values was a turning point. It allowed her to embrace her identity more fully, fostering a relationship built on mutual respect and understanding.

## Cultural Barriers to Love

Despite the joy that love can bring, cultural barriers often pose significant challenges. In Myanmar, where conservative values prevail, LGBTQ relationships can be met with hostility or disapproval. The fear of public scrutiny can lead to secretive relationships, preventing individuals from fully expressing their love. This secrecy can create a sense of shame and isolation, complicating the emotional landscape of LGBTQ individuals.

$$\text{Relationship Quality} = g(\text{Openness, Support, Cultural Acceptance}) \qquad (10)$$

Here, the quality of a relationship is a function of openness, support from the community, and cultural acceptance. When these factors are lacking, the relationship may struggle to thrive.

## Building a Supportive Community

The role of community in finding love cannot be understated. For many LGBTQ individuals, connecting with others who share similar experiences can provide a vital support network. This community can offer encouragement, resources, and a sense of belonging that is often missing in broader society.

Wai Wai found solace in LGBTQ support groups, where she met individuals who understood her struggles. These connections not only provided emotional support but also opened doors to potential romantic relationships. The power of community is encapsulated in the idea that love can be both a personal journey and a collective experience.

## The Joy of Love

Despite the challenges, the joy of finding love is a profound experience. For Wai Wai, her relationship became a source of strength and resilience. Love provided a refuge from societal pressures, allowing her to express her true self. The emotional highs and lows of romantic relationships are universal, transcending cultural boundaries.

In this context, love acts as a catalyst for personal growth. It encourages individuals to confront their fears, embrace their identities, and advocate for their rights. The act of loving and being loved can empower individuals to challenge societal norms and push for greater acceptance.

## Conclusion

Finding love as an LGBTQ individual in Myanmar is a multifaceted journey marked by challenges and triumphs. For Wai Wai Nu, the path to love was shaped by her experiences of self-discovery, the support of her community, and the courage to embrace her identity. As she navigated the complexities of relationships, she not only found love but also a deeper understanding of herself and her place in the world. Ultimately, love serves as both a personal refuge and a powerful force for social change, inspiring others to pursue their own paths to acceptance and happiness.

## Exploring Gender Identity

In the journey of self-discovery, the exploration of gender identity stands as a pivotal chapter, particularly for individuals navigating the complexities of a traditional society like Myanmar. Gender identity, defined as a personal conception of oneself as male, female, a blend of both, or neither, can be deeply influenced by cultural, social, and familial expectations. For many, including Wai Wai Nu, understanding one's gender identity is not merely an internal process but a confrontation with external realities that can either affirm or challenge one's sense of self.

## Theoretical Frameworks

Several theoretical frameworks provide insight into the exploration of gender identity. Judith Butler's theory of gender performativity posits that gender is not an inherent quality but rather a series of performances that individuals engage in based on societal expectations. This perspective allows for a nuanced understanding of how individuals like Wai Wai navigate their identities in a conservative society where traditional gender roles are rigidly enforced.

Moreover, the concept of intersectionality, introduced by Kimberlé Crenshaw, emphasizes that gender identity cannot be understood in isolation from other identities such as ethnicity, sexuality, and class. In the context of Myanmar, where ethnic diversity is significant, the intersection of these identities complicates the exploration of gender. For instance, Wai Wai's identity as a Rohingya woman adds layers of complexity, as she must navigate both gender and ethnic discrimination.

## Personal Experiences and Societal Context

Wai Wai's journey of exploring her gender identity began in her early adolescence, a time when societal expectations regarding femininity were pronounced. In a society where traditional gender roles dictate behavior, appearance, and aspirations, the pressure to conform can be overwhelming. The early signs of her non-conformity were met with confusion and resistance from her peers and family, leading to feelings of isolation.

The cultural backdrop of Myanmar, steeped in patriarchal values, often relegates women to submissive roles, leaving little room for the expression of diverse gender identities. For Wai Wai, the realization that her gender identity did not align with societal norms was both liberating and terrifying. The fear of rejection and violence loomed large, as stories of individuals facing severe repercussions for defying gender norms circulated within her community.

## The Role of Education and Awareness

Education plays a crucial role in shaping one's understanding of gender identity. In Myanmar, access to LGBTQ-inclusive education is limited, resulting in a lack of awareness about gender diversity. Workshops and training programs that focus on gender identity can empower individuals to embrace their authentic selves. For Wai Wai, participating in such initiatives not only provided her with the language to articulate her experiences but also connected her with a community of like-minded individuals.

The importance of allyship cannot be overstated in this context. Allies, including supportive family members, friends, and educators, can create safe spaces for exploration and expression. Wai Wai found solace in friendships with individuals who understood her struggles, allowing her to express her gender identity without fear of judgment. This support network became a vital lifeline, reinforcing her sense of belonging and acceptance.

## Challenges Faced

Despite the progress made in understanding gender identity, challenges persist. The stigma surrounding non-binary and gender non-conforming identities often leads to discrimination and violence. In Myanmar, where traditional gender norms are deeply entrenched, individuals who do not conform to these expectations face heightened risks. Wai Wai encountered instances of harassment and exclusion, both in social settings and within educational institutions, illustrating the pervasive nature of gender-based discrimination.

Additionally, the legal framework in Myanmar does not recognize diverse gender identities, leaving individuals vulnerable to systemic discrimination. The lack of legal protections exacerbates the challenges faced by those exploring their gender identity, as they navigate a landscape fraught with obstacles. Advocacy for legal reforms that recognize and protect diverse gender identities is crucial in fostering an environment where individuals can explore their identities freely.

## Embracing Fluidity and Authenticity

As Wai Wai continued her exploration of gender identity, she began to embrace the fluidity of her identity. Understanding that gender is not a binary construct but rather a spectrum allowed her to redefine her sense of self on her own terms. This journey towards authenticity is often marked by moments of joy and pain, as individuals navigate the complexities of self-acceptance in a world that often demands conformity.

The celebration of gender diversity is essential in challenging societal norms and fostering acceptance. By sharing her story and engaging in activism, Wai Wai contributes to a broader movement that seeks to dismantle the rigid structures of gender identity. Her experiences serve as a powerful reminder that the exploration of gender identity is not only a personal journey but also a collective struggle for recognition and rights.

## Conclusion

The exploration of gender identity is a profound and multifaceted journey, particularly for individuals like Wai Wai Nu in Myanmar. By understanding the theoretical frameworks, acknowledging personal experiences, and recognizing the societal context, we can appreciate the complexities involved in this exploration. As society continues to evolve, it is imperative to advocate for inclusive education, legal protections, and supportive networks that empower individuals to embrace their authentic selves. The journey towards self-acceptance and authenticity is not only vital for personal well-being but also essential for the advancement of LGBTQ rights in Myanmar and beyond.

## The Intersectionality of LGBTQ and Ethnic Identity

The concept of intersectionality, first coined by legal scholar Kimberlé Crenshaw, refers to how various social identities, such as race, gender, sexuality, and ethnicity, intersect to create unique modes of discrimination and privilege. In the context of LGBTQ activism in Myanmar, the intersectionality of LGBTQ identities and ethnic identities reveals complex layers of marginalization that individuals face, particularly for those belonging to ethnic minorities.

### Understanding Intersectionality

Intersectionality posits that individuals do not experience discrimination or privilege in isolation; rather, their experiences are shaped by the interplay of multiple identities. This framework is crucial for understanding the challenges faced by LGBTQ individuals in Myanmar, where ethnic identity plays a significant role in social dynamics. For instance, the Rohingya, an ethnic minority group in Myanmar, face severe discrimination and violence, which is compounded by their sexual orientation or gender identity if they identify as LGBTQ.

## Cultural Context

Myanmar is home to a diverse array of ethnic groups, each with its own cultural norms and values. The predominant Burman culture often marginalizes ethnic minorities, and this marginalization is intensified for LGBTQ individuals within these groups. For example, within the Kachin community, traditional beliefs may dictate strict gender roles, leaving little room for the acceptance of non-heteronormative identities. This cultural backdrop can lead to a heightened sense of isolation and fear among LGBTQ individuals who also belong to ethnic minorities.

## Challenges Faced by LGBTQ Ethnic Minorities

LGBTQ individuals from ethnic minority backgrounds often encounter a dual burden of discrimination. They may face homophobia and transphobia from the broader society while simultaneously grappling with ethnic discrimination within their own communities. This results in a lack of safe spaces where they can express their identities freely. For instance, a gay Kachin man may feel rejected not only by his family due to his sexuality but also by the LGBTQ community, which may prioritize the struggles of the Burman identity over those of ethnic minorities.

Moreover, the intersection of LGBTQ and ethnic identities can lead to unique health disparities. Ethnic minority LGBTQ individuals may have limited access to healthcare services that are both culturally competent and LGBTQ-inclusive. This can exacerbate mental health issues, as individuals may feel alienated from both their ethnic communities and the LGBTQ community.

## Activism and Solidarity

Activism within the LGBTQ community in Myanmar must be inclusive of ethnic identities to address these intersecting issues. Advocacy efforts that recognize the unique challenges faced by LGBTQ individuals from various ethnic backgrounds can foster solidarity and collective action. For instance, initiatives that highlight the stories of LGBTQ ethnic minorities can help raise awareness and promote understanding within both the LGBTQ community and the broader society.

Collaborations between LGBTQ activists and ethnic rights organizations can also strengthen the movement. By uniting under the common goal of fighting for equality, these groups can amplify their voices and challenge the systemic discrimination that exists at the intersections of ethnicity and sexual orientation.

## Case Studies and Examples

A poignant example of intersectionality in action is the case of Wai Wai Nu, an LGBTQ activist of Rohingya descent. Her work exemplifies the struggle for both LGBTQ rights and ethnic minority rights in Myanmar. Through her activism, she has brought attention to the plight of LGBTQ individuals within the Rohingya community, showcasing how their experiences are often overlooked in broader discussions about LGBTQ rights.

Another example is the formation of grassroots organizations that focus on providing support to LGBTQ ethnic minorities. These organizations often conduct workshops and training sessions that address the unique cultural sensitivities of ethnic communities while promoting LGBTQ rights. Such initiatives have proven effective in building trust and fostering dialogue within these communities.

## Theoretical Implications

The intersectionality of LGBTQ and ethnic identities in Myanmar challenges traditional frameworks of human rights advocacy, which often treat identities as discrete categories. Instead, an intersectional approach recognizes the fluidity and complexity of identity, urging activists to consider how various forms of discrimination interconnect. This theoretical shift is essential for developing comprehensive strategies that address the needs of all marginalized groups.

In conclusion, the intersectionality of LGBTQ and ethnic identity is a critical aspect of the struggle for rights and recognition in Myanmar. Understanding this intersectionality allows for a more nuanced approach to activism, one that honors the diverse experiences of individuals and fosters a more inclusive movement. By embracing intersectionality, LGBTQ activists can work towards a future where all individuals, regardless of their ethnic background or sexual orientation, can live authentically and with dignity.

$$\text{Intersectionality} = \text{LGBTQ Identity} + \text{Ethnic Identity} + \text{Cultural Context} + \text{Social Dynam}$$
$$(11)$$

# Overcoming Stereotypes and Preconceptions

Overcoming stereotypes and preconceptions is a critical aspect of Wai Wai Nu's journey as an LGBTQ activist in Myanmar. In a society steeped in traditional values and conservative norms, the challenge of dismantling deeply entrenched biases can be overwhelming. This section explores the theoretical frameworks surrounding stereotypes, the problems they pose, and real-life examples of overcoming these barriers.

## Theoretical Frameworks

Stereotypes are cognitive structures that influence how individuals perceive and interact with others. According to [?], stereotypes can be defined as "the mental image or impression of a group of people." They often lead to generalizations that can be harmful and reductive. The **Social Identity Theory** posits that individuals categorize themselves and others into groups, which can foster in-group favoritism and out-group discrimination [?].

In the context of LGBTQ identities in Myanmar, stereotypes often manifest as assumptions about behavior, lifestyle choices, and moral character. For instance, the stereotype that LGBTQ individuals are promiscuous or morally corrupt can lead to societal ostracism and discrimination. This is compounded by cultural narratives that frame homosexuality as a Western import, further alienating LGBTQ individuals from their cultural roots.

## Challenges Faced

The challenges of overcoming stereotypes are multifaceted:

+ **Social Stigma:** LGBTQ individuals often face social stigma that affects their mental health and well-being. The fear of being labeled or judged can deter individuals from expressing their true selves, leading to internalized homophobia.

+ **Media Representation:** The portrayal of LGBTQ individuals in media can perpetuate harmful stereotypes. In Myanmar, media often sensationalizes LGBTQ stories, framing them in a negative light, which reinforces existing prejudices.

+ **Cultural Norms:** Traditional beliefs about gender roles and sexuality create an environment where LGBTQ identities are seen as deviant. This cultural backdrop complicates the process of acceptance and understanding.

## Real-Life Examples of Overcoming Stereotypes

Despite these challenges, Wai Wai Nu and her peers have made significant strides in overcoming stereotypes and preconceptions:

**Community Engagement** Wai Wai Nu emphasizes the importance of community engagement in breaking down stereotypes. By organizing events that celebrate LGBTQ culture, she creates opportunities for dialogue and understanding. For example, the annual Pride celebrations in Yangon have become a platform for visibility, allowing LGBTQ individuals to share their stories and experiences with a broader audience.

**Education and Awareness** Education plays a pivotal role in changing perceptions. Workshops and training sessions aimed at schools and community organizations have been instrumental in dispelling myths about LGBTQ individuals. By providing accurate information and fostering discussions about diversity, activists challenge preconceived notions and promote acceptance.

**Personal Narratives** Sharing personal stories is a powerful tool for combating stereotypes. Wai Wai Nu's own journey of self-acceptance and activism serves as an inspiration to others. By publicly sharing her experiences, she humanizes the LGBTQ community, encouraging others to see beyond stereotypes. This aligns with the **Contact Hypothesis**, which suggests that increased interaction between groups can reduce prejudice [?].

## The Role of Allies

Allies play a crucial role in supporting LGBTQ individuals in their fight against stereotypes. Engaging with allies from various sectors, including education, politics, and healthcare, helps to amplify LGBTQ voices and challenges the status quo. For instance, collaborations with human rights organizations have led to increased visibility and support for LGBTQ rights in Myanmar, fostering a more inclusive environment.

## Conclusion

Overcoming stereotypes and preconceptions is an ongoing battle for LGBTQ activists like Wai Wai Nu. Through community engagement, education, personal storytelling, and allyship, they are paving the way for a more inclusive society. While challenges remain, the collective efforts of individuals and organizations are gradually dismantling the barriers of prejudice, fostering a culture of acceptance and understanding in Myanmar.

## Embracing Queerness in a Conservative Society

In a society deeply rooted in traditional values and norms, embracing queerness presents a formidable challenge. Myanmar, with its rich cultural tapestry, often intertwines conservative ideologies with the prevailing social fabric. This section explores the complexities faced by LGBTQ individuals in Myanmar as they navigate their identities within a conservative context, drawing upon relevant theories, real-life examples, and the broader implications of such experiences.

## Theoretical Framework

To understand the dynamics of queerness in a conservative society, we can apply Judith Butler's theory of gender performativity, which posits that gender is not an inherent identity but rather a series of acts and performances shaped by societal expectations. In conservative societies, these performances are strictly regulated, leading to the marginalization of those who do not conform to normative gender roles. This framework allows us to analyze how LGBTQ individuals in Myanmar negotiate their identities against the backdrop of societal expectations.

## Cultural Context and Identity

The cultural context in Myanmar is predominantly influenced by Buddhism, which often emphasizes traditional gender roles and heterosexual relationships. As a result, LGBTQ individuals may face significant pressure to conform to these expectations. The intersection of cultural norms and religious beliefs can create a hostile environment for those who identify as queer. For instance, individuals may experience familial rejection or societal ostracization when they express their true selves.

$$C = \frac{S}{R} \tag{12}$$

Where $C$ represents the cultural acceptance of queerness, $S$ signifies the societal support for LGBTQ individuals, and $R$ denotes the resistance from traditional norms. As such, a low $C$ value indicates a challenging environment for queer individuals, often leading to internalized homophobia and a struggle for self-acceptance.

## Personal Narratives

Wai Wai Nu, a prominent LGBTQ activist in Myanmar, exemplifies the journey of embracing queerness in a conservative society. Despite the pervasive stigma, she found strength in her identity and used her experiences to advocate for change. Her story resonates with many who grapple with similar challenges. In her early years, she faced immense pressure to conform to societal expectations, often leading to a fear of rejection and isolation.

An example of this is the story of a young gay man from Yangon, who, after coming out to his family, faced severe backlash and was forced to leave home. This narrative highlights the real dangers LGBTQ individuals face when embracing their identities in a conservative society. The psychological impact of such experiences can be profound, often leading to anxiety, depression, and a sense of alienation.

## Community Support and Resilience

Despite the challenges, the LGBTQ community in Myanmar has shown remarkable resilience. Grassroots organizations have emerged, providing safe spaces for individuals to explore their identities and connect with others. Events such as pride parades and awareness campaigns serve as platforms for visibility and acceptance. These initiatives challenge the status quo and create opportunities for dialogue around queerness in a conservative context.

For instance, the annual Yangon Pride event has become a symbol of resistance and empowerment for the LGBTQ community. It draws attention to the struggles faced by queer individuals and fosters a sense of solidarity among participants. Through visibility, the community seeks to dismantle stereotypes and promote understanding.

## Intersectionality and Queerness

The concept of intersectionality, coined by Kimberlé Crenshaw, is crucial in understanding the diverse experiences of LGBTQ individuals in Myanmar. Many face compounded discrimination due to their ethnicity, religion, and socio-economic status. For example, queer individuals from ethnic minority groups may encounter additional barriers, as their identities intersect with systemic inequalities.

By embracing queerness within the framework of intersectionality, activists can address the unique challenges faced by diverse members of the LGBTQ community. This approach fosters inclusivity and ensures that all voices are heard in the fight for rights and recognition.

## Conclusion

Embracing queerness in a conservative society like Myanmar requires immense courage and resilience. Through personal narratives, community support, and the application of theoretical frameworks, we can better understand the complexities of this journey. As activists like Wai Wai Nu continue to advocate for change, the hope for a more inclusive society grows stronger. The path to acceptance may be fraught with challenges, but the determination to embrace one's identity remains a powerful catalyst for social transformation.

# Advocating for LGBTQ Rights

## Becoming an Activist

The journey of becoming an activist is often a transformative experience, marked by personal growth, societal challenges, and the relentless pursuit of justice. For Wai Wai Nu, the path to activism was not merely a choice but a necessity born from the harsh realities of living in a society that marginalized her identity. Activism is fundamentally about advocating for change, but it also involves understanding the underlying structures of oppression and the ways in which they manifest in everyday life.

## Understanding Activism

At its core, activism is the act of taking action to effect social change. It can take many forms, including protests, advocacy, education, and community organizing. Theoretical frameworks, such as the *Social Movement Theory*, provide insight into how movements emerge, grow, and achieve their goals. This theory posits that social movements arise in response to perceived injustices and are sustained by collective action and shared identities among participants.

Wai Wai's activism began with a realization that her identity as a member of the LGBTQ community in Myanmar was intrinsically linked to broader issues of human rights. According to the *Intersectionality Theory*, individuals experience overlapping systems of discrimination, which in Wai Wai's case included gender, sexual orientation, and ethnic identity. This understanding propelled her into the world of activism, where she sought to address the multifaceted nature of oppression faced by LGBTQ individuals in Myanmar.

## The Initial Steps

The initial steps towards activism are often filled with uncertainty and fear. For Wai Wai, these emotions were compounded by the societal norms of Myanmar, where traditional values often clash with modern understandings of gender and sexuality. The first challenge was to confront her own fears and insecurities about being openly LGBTQ in a conservative society. This internal struggle is a common experience among activists, as they grapple with the potential backlash from their communities and families.

Wai Wai found inspiration in the stories of other activists who had dared to stand up against injustice. This sense of solidarity is crucial in activism, as it fosters a community of support that can help individuals navigate the challenges they face. The act of sharing personal stories can also serve as a powerful tool for advocacy, as it humanizes the issues at stake and creates empathy among allies.

## Building a Network

As Wai Wai began to embrace her identity, she sought out like-minded individuals who shared her passion for LGBTQ rights. Building a network of allies and supporters is essential for any activist, as it amplifies their voice and increases their impact. In Myanmar, this meant connecting with local LGBTQ groups, human rights organizations, and even sympathetic individuals within the political sphere.

The importance of coalition-building cannot be overstated. By collaborating with other marginalized communities, activists can create a more inclusive movement that addresses the diverse needs of all individuals. For instance, Wai Wai engaged with women's rights groups to highlight the intersectionality of gender and sexual orientation, thereby broadening the scope of her activism.

## Education and Awareness

Education plays a pivotal role in activism. For Wai Wai, becoming an activist meant not only advocating for LGBTQ rights but also educating herself and others about the importance of acceptance and understanding. This involves challenging stereotypes and misconceptions that perpetuate discrimination. Workshops, seminars, and community discussions became vital tools for spreading awareness about LGBTQ issues in Myanmar.

One of the significant barriers to acceptance is the lack of accurate information about LGBTQ identities. Activists like Wai Wai have taken it upon themselves to combat misinformation through educational initiatives. By providing resources and creating safe spaces for dialogue, they empower individuals to confront their biases and embrace diversity.

## The Role of Visibility

Visibility is a double-edged sword in the realm of activism. While being visible can empower individuals and foster community, it also exposes them to risks and vulnerabilities. For Wai Wai, becoming an activist meant stepping into the public eye, which required immense courage. The power of visibility lies in its ability to challenge societal norms and inspire others to join the movement.

Wai Wai's participation in pride events and public demonstrations not only raised awareness but also provided a sense of belonging for many individuals who felt isolated in their struggles. The act of being visible can also serve as a form of resistance against oppressive systems, as it challenges the status quo and demands recognition for marginalized identities.

## Facing Challenges

The path of activism is fraught with challenges, and Wai Wai's journey was no exception. Activists often face threats, harassment, and even legal repercussions for their work. In Myanmar, where LGBTQ identities are criminalized, the stakes are particularly high. This reality necessitates a strong support system and resilience in the face of adversity.

Wai Wai encountered numerous obstacles, from societal backlash to personal threats. However, these challenges only fueled her determination to fight for change. The concept of *resilience* is crucial in activism; it enables individuals to withstand pressures and continue their advocacy despite setbacks.

## Creating Change

Ultimately, becoming an activist is about creating change—both within oneself and in the broader society. For Wai Wai, this meant not only advocating for legal reforms but also fostering a culture of acceptance and understanding within her community. Activism is a long-term commitment that requires patience, persistence, and a willingness to adapt to changing circumstances.

Wai Wai's journey exemplifies the profound impact that one individual can have on a movement. By embracing her identity and standing up for her rights, she has inspired countless others to do the same. The ripple effects of her activism extend beyond Myanmar, contributing to a global dialogue about LGBTQ rights and the importance of intersectional advocacy.

In conclusion, becoming an activist is a multifaceted journey that involves personal growth, community building, and the relentless pursuit of justice. Wai Wai Nu's story serves as a testament to the power of activism in challenging societal norms and advocating for the rights of marginalized communities. As she continues to fight for LGBTQ rights in Myanmar, her journey reminds us that activism is not just a destination but a lifelong commitment to creating a more equitable world.

## The Power of Visibility

In the realm of LGBTQ activism, visibility serves as a potent catalyst for change, particularly in a society like Myanmar, where cultural norms often suppress open discussions about gender and sexual identity. The act of being visible—whether through personal testimonies, public demonstrations, or media representation—creates a ripple effect that can challenge stereotypes, foster acceptance, and inspire others to embrace their identities. This section delves into the multifaceted power of visibility, examining its theoretical underpinnings, the challenges it presents, and real-world examples from the LGBTQ movement in Myanmar.

### Theoretical Foundations of Visibility

The concept of visibility in LGBTQ activism can be understood through several theoretical lenses. One prominent framework is the *Queer Theory*, which posits that identities are fluid and socially constructed. Queer theorists argue that visibility is crucial in destabilizing normative understandings of gender and sexuality, allowing for a broader spectrum of identities to emerge. Judith Butler, a leading figure in queer theory, emphasizes that "gender is performative," suggesting that visibility can challenge and redefine societal norms through the very act of being seen.

Another relevant theory is *Social Identity Theory*, which posits that individuals derive a sense of self from their membership in social groups. Visibility can enhance group identity and cohesion among LGBTQ individuals, fostering a sense of belonging and community. When individuals see others like themselves represented in society, it can validate their experiences and encourage them to embrace their identities.

### Challenges of Visibility

Despite its transformative potential, the pursuit of visibility is fraught with challenges, particularly in conservative societies like Myanmar. The fear of backlash—ranging from social ostracism to physical violence—can deter individuals from coming out or participating in public activism. This fear is compounded by the deeply entrenched cultural and religious beliefs that often demonize LGBTQ identities.

Moreover, the visibility of LGBTQ individuals can sometimes lead to tokenism, where individuals are used as symbols of diversity without substantive change in policies or societal attitudes. This phenomenon can undermine the authenticity of the movement and perpetuate stereotypes rather than dismantling them.

## Real-World Examples

In Myanmar, the power of visibility has been harnessed in various ways, leading to significant strides in LGBTQ rights. One notable example is the annual Pride Parade in Yangon, which has become a symbol of resistance and community. The parade not only provides a platform for LGBTQ individuals to express their identities but also attracts media attention, sparking conversations about LGBTQ rights in the broader society.

The visibility of LGBTQ activists like Wai Wai Nu has also played a crucial role in this movement. Her public advocacy and personal narrative have inspired many to embrace their identities and take a stand against discrimination. By sharing her story through various media outlets, Wai Wai has illuminated the struggles faced by LGBTQ individuals in Myanmar, thereby humanizing the issues at stake and garnering empathy from the public.

Furthermore, collaborations with international LGBTQ organizations have amplified the voices of Myanmar's LGBTQ community on a global scale. By participating in international conferences and sharing their experiences, activists have brought attention to the unique challenges faced in Myanmar, fostering solidarity with global movements.

## The Ripple Effect of Visibility

The impact of visibility extends beyond individual empowerment; it has the potential to influence societal attitudes and policies. When LGBTQ individuals are visible in media, politics, and social spheres, they challenge the prevailing narratives that often marginalize them. This visibility can lead to increased awareness and understanding among the general public, paving the way for greater acceptance and legal reforms.

For instance, the portrayal of LGBTQ characters in local media can help normalize diverse identities and challenge harmful stereotypes. As audiences engage with these narratives, they may begin to question their own biases and assumptions, leading to a more inclusive society.

## Conclusion

In conclusion, the power of visibility in LGBTQ activism cannot be overstated. It serves as a tool for empowerment, a means of challenging societal norms, and a catalyst for change. While the journey toward visibility is fraught with challenges, the stories of activists like Wai Wai Nu highlight the profound impact that visibility can have on individuals and communities. As the LGBTQ movement in Myanmar continues to evolve, embracing visibility will be crucial in the fight for equality and acceptance. The more visible the LGBTQ community becomes, the closer society moves toward a future where diversity is celebrated and all individuals can live authentically and freely.

## Organizing LGBTQ Community Events

Organizing LGBTQ community events is a vital aspect of advocacy that fosters visibility, solidarity, and empowerment within the community. These events serve not only as platforms for celebration but also as critical spaces for education, awareness, and mobilization. In Myanmar, where societal norms often marginalize LGBTQ individuals, the organization of such events becomes even more significant.

## The Importance of Community Events

Community events play a crucial role in building a sense of belonging among LGBTQ individuals. They create an environment where people can express their identities freely and connect with others who share similar experiences. According to social identity theory, individuals derive a sense of self from their group memberships, which can enhance their self-esteem and overall well-being [?]. In Myanmar, where cultural and legal barriers often impede LGBTQ visibility, these events can challenge stereotypes and promote acceptance.

## Types of Events

LGBTQ community events can take various forms, including:

- **Pride Parades and Festivals:** These large-scale events celebrate LGBTQ identities and promote visibility. They often feature performances, speeches, and community booths.

- **Workshops and Seminars:** Educational events that focus on topics such as health, legal rights, and advocacy strategies. These sessions empower participants with knowledge and skills.

- **Support Groups:** Regular meetings that provide a safe space for individuals to share experiences, seek advice, and build community support.

- **Art and Cultural Events:** Exhibitions, film screenings, and performances that highlight LGBTQ culture and issues, fostering creativity and expression.

## Challenges in Organizing Events

Despite the importance of these events, organizing them in Myanmar presents unique challenges:

- **Legal Restrictions:** Homosexuality remains criminalized in Myanmar, which can create legal risks for organizers and participants. This environment may lead to self-censorship and reluctance to participate in public events.

- **Social Stigma:** Deep-rooted prejudices against LGBTQ individuals can result in backlash from conservative segments of society. Organizers must navigate potential threats and hostility.

- **Resource Limitations:** Many LGBTQ organizations in Myanmar operate with limited funding and resources, making it difficult to host large-scale events or outreach programs.

- **Safety Concerns:** Ensuring the safety of participants is paramount. Organizers must consider security measures, particularly when events are public or high-profile.

## Strategies for Successful Events

To overcome these challenges, LGBTQ activists in Myanmar have developed several strategies for organizing successful community events:

- **Building Alliances:** Collaborating with local NGOs, human rights organizations, and sympathetic political figures can provide additional support and legitimacy to events.

+ **Creating Safe Spaces:** Ensuring that venues are secure and welcoming is essential. This may involve private locations or pre-arranged spaces that prioritize participant safety.

+ **Utilizing Social Media:** Leveraging social media platforms allows organizers to promote events discreetly while reaching a broader audience. It also serves as a tool for community engagement and mobilization.

+ **Engaging the Community:** Involving community members in the planning process fosters ownership and encourages participation. This can include soliciting feedback, volunteers, and local talent for events.

## Examples of Successful Events

Several successful LGBTQ community events in Myanmar exemplify effective organizing:

+ **Yangon Pride:** An annual celebration that has garnered attention and participation from both the LGBTQ community and allies. The event includes a parade, workshops, and cultural performances, showcasing the diversity of the LGBTQ experience in Myanmar.

+ **Queer Film Festival:** A festival that screens LGBTQ-themed films, providing a platform for storytelling and discussion. This event not only entertains but also educates audiences about LGBTQ issues and experiences.

+ **Health Awareness Days:** Events focused on LGBTQ health, offering free screenings, educational materials, and discussions about sexual health and rights. These events address critical health disparities within the community.

## Conclusion

Organizing LGBTQ community events in Myanmar is a powerful tool for advocacy and empowerment. Despite the challenges posed by societal norms and legal restrictions, these events foster connection, education, and visibility. Through strategic planning, community engagement, and collaboration, activists can create impactful events that not only celebrate LGBTQ identities but also advocate for change in a conservative society. The ongoing efforts of individuals like Wai Wai Nu exemplify the resilience and determination of the LGBTQ community in

Myanmar, paving the way for future generations to thrive in a more inclusive environment.

## Fighting Against Discrimination

Fighting against discrimination is a cornerstone of LGBTQ activism, particularly in a country like Myanmar, where deeply rooted cultural and societal norms often perpetuate prejudice and inequality. Discrimination against LGBTQ individuals manifests in various forms, including social ostracism, legal injustices, and violence. This section explores the strategies employed by activists, the theoretical frameworks that underpin their efforts, and the real-world examples that illustrate the ongoing struggle against discrimination.

### Theoretical Frameworks

Understanding discrimination requires a multi-faceted approach that considers intersectionality, social justice, and human rights. Intersectionality, a term coined by Kimberlé Crenshaw, emphasizes that individuals experience discrimination in overlapping and interdependent ways. For LGBTQ individuals in Myanmar, their identities intersect with ethnicity, religion, and socio-economic status, compounding the discrimination they face.

Social justice theory advocates for equitable treatment and the dismantling of systemic barriers that marginalize certain groups. This framework encourages activists to challenge not only individual acts of discrimination but also the societal structures that uphold inequality. The Universal Declaration of Human Rights (UDHR) serves as a foundational document in the fight against discrimination, asserting that all human beings are entitled to rights and freedoms without distinction of any kind.

### Identifying Discrimination

Discrimination against LGBTQ individuals in Myanmar is often institutionalized, with laws that criminalize same-sex relationships and fail to protect individuals from hate crimes. Article 377 of the Myanmar Penal Code, for instance, criminalizes consensual same-sex conduct, leading to widespread fear and silence among LGBTQ individuals. This legal framework reinforces societal prejudices, making it difficult for individuals to seek justice when they face discrimination.

Activists have documented various forms of discrimination, including:

- **Employment Discrimination:** Many LGBTQ individuals face job loss or discrimination in hiring processes due to their sexual orientation or gender identity.

- **Healthcare Discrimination:** LGBTQ individuals often encounter healthcare providers who lack sensitivity or knowledge regarding LGBTQ issues, leading to inadequate care.

- **Social Stigmatization:** LGBTQ individuals frequently face harassment and violence in public spaces, contributing to a culture of fear and isolation.

## Strategies for Combatting Discrimination

Activists employ various strategies to combat discrimination, focusing on advocacy, education, and community engagement.

**Advocacy**   Advocacy efforts aim to influence policy and legal reform. Activists work tirelessly to engage lawmakers and push for the repeal of discriminatory laws. For instance, campaigns have been organized to raise awareness about the implications of Article 377, advocating for its repeal as a necessary step towards equality.

**Education**   Education plays a critical role in combating discrimination. Activists conduct workshops and training programs aimed at informing both the LGBTQ community and the general public about LGBTQ rights and issues. These initiatives help to debunk myths and stereotypes that fuel discrimination. For example, community-led initiatives have successfully reached schools, educating students about the importance of acceptance and inclusivity.

**Community Engagement**   Building a strong and supportive community is essential for fighting discrimination. Activists have established safe spaces where LGBTQ individuals can connect, share experiences, and find solidarity. Community centers serve as hubs for organizing events, providing resources, and fostering a sense of belonging. For instance, the establishment of LGBTQ community centers in Yangon has provided a platform for individuals to gather, seek support, and engage in activism.

## Real-World Examples

Several notable examples illustrate the effectiveness of these strategies in fighting discrimination.

**Pride Events**   Despite the risks, LGBTQ activists in Myanmar have organized pride events to promote visibility and celebrate diversity. These events challenge societal norms and provide a platform for LGBTQ individuals to express themselves. The first pride parade in Yangon, held in 2019, was a significant milestone, drawing attention to the issues faced by the LGBTQ community and fostering a sense of unity among participants.

**Legal Challenges**   Activists have also pursued legal challenges against discriminatory practices. In 2020, a group of LGBTQ activists collaborated with human rights lawyers to challenge the constitutionality of Article 377. Their efforts highlighted the need for legal reforms and garnered international attention, putting pressure on the government to reconsider its stance on LGBTQ rights.

## Conclusion

Fighting against discrimination is an ongoing battle for LGBTQ activists in Myanmar. Through advocacy, education, and community engagement, they are working to dismantle the barriers that perpetuate inequality. The intersectionality of their identities adds complexity to their struggle, but it also fuels a powerful movement for change. As activists continue to challenge discriminatory laws and societal norms, they pave the way for a more inclusive and equitable future for all individuals, regardless of their sexual orientation or gender identity. The fight against discrimination is not just a fight for LGBTQ rights; it is a fight for human rights, dignity, and justice for all.

## Speaking Out Against Homophobia and Transphobia

In the struggle for LGBTQ rights, speaking out against homophobia and transphobia is not merely an act of defiance; it is a fundamental necessity for fostering a society that values diversity and inclusion. Homophobia and transphobia are rooted in a complex web of cultural, social, and psychological factors that perpetuate discrimination and violence against LGBTQ individuals. Understanding these dynamics is crucial for effective advocacy.

## Theoretical Framework

Homophobia can be understood through the lens of *social identity theory*, which posits that individuals derive a significant part of their identity from the social groups to which they belong. When societal norms dictate that heterosexuality is the only acceptable orientation, any deviation from this norm can lead to fear and hostility toward LGBTQ individuals. This fear often manifests as homophobia, resulting in systemic discrimination.

Similarly, *gender identity theory* explains transphobia as a reaction to non-conformity to traditional gender roles. The rigidity of gender binaries creates an environment where those who identify as transgender or gender non-conforming are marginalized and subjected to violence and discrimination.

## Problems Arising from Homophobia and Transphobia

The consequences of homophobia and transphobia are severe and pervasive. LGBTQ individuals often face:

- **Mental Health Issues:** Studies have shown that individuals who experience discrimination due to their sexual orientation or gender identity are at a higher risk for depression, anxiety, and suicidal ideation. The *American Psychological Association* has noted that minority stress—resulting from societal stigma—significantly impacts mental well-being.

- **Violence and Hate Crimes:** The LGBTQ community is disproportionately affected by hate crimes. According to the *FBI's Hate Crime Statistics*, a significant percentage of hate crimes are motivated by sexual orientation and gender identity, highlighting the urgent need for advocacy and protective measures.

- **Economic Disparities:** Discrimination in the workplace can lead to economic instability for LGBTQ individuals. Many face barriers to employment, unequal pay, and lack of access to benefits, which perpetuates cycles of poverty.

- **Social Isolation:** Homophobia and transphobia can lead to social ostracism, where LGBTQ individuals find themselves alienated from their communities, families, and support systems, exacerbating feelings of loneliness and despair.

## Advocacy Strategies

To combat these issues, activists like Wai Wai Nu have employed various strategies to speak out against homophobia and transphobia:

+ **Public Awareness Campaigns:** Utilizing social media platforms and traditional media, activists have launched campaigns aimed at educating the public about LGBTQ issues. These campaigns often include personal stories that humanize the struggles faced by LGBTQ individuals, fostering empathy and understanding.

+ **Community Workshops:** Organizing workshops that focus on LGBTQ rights, inclusivity, and allyship can empower individuals to challenge their own biases and become advocates for change. These workshops often include training on how to respond to homophobic or transphobic remarks in everyday situations.

+ **Engagement with Policymakers:** Activists have engaged with local and national leaders to advocate for laws that protect LGBTQ rights. This includes lobbying for hate crime legislation and anti-discrimination laws that explicitly include sexual orientation and gender identity.

+ **Coalition Building:** Forming alliances with other marginalized groups enhances the impact of advocacy efforts. By addressing the intersectionality of various forms of discrimination, activists can create a more inclusive movement that resonates with a broader audience.

## Real-World Examples

In Myanmar, where cultural and religious conservatism often fuels homophobia and transphobia, activists have faced significant challenges. For instance, during the 2019 LGBTQ Pride Parade in Yangon, participants encountered both support and backlash. Activists used the event as an opportunity to speak out against discrimination, sharing stories of individuals who had faced violence and rejection due to their sexual orientation. This visibility was crucial in challenging societal norms and promoting acceptance.

Internationally, movements like the *It Gets Better Project* have demonstrated the power of collective voices in combating homophobia and transphobia. By sharing personal narratives of resilience and hope, these campaigns have inspired countless individuals to embrace their identities and challenge the stigma surrounding LGBTQ lives.

## Conclusion

Speaking out against homophobia and transphobia is an essential component of the fight for LGBTQ rights.    By understanding the underlying theories, recognizing the problems, and implementing effective advocacy strategies, activists can create a safer and more inclusive society for all. The work of individuals like Wai Wai Nu exemplifies the courage and determination needed to confront discrimination head-on, inspiring future generations to continue the struggle for equality and acceptance.

## Engaging with Media and Politics

Engaging with media and politics is crucial for LGBTQ activists seeking to amplify their voices and advocate for change. In Myanmar, where traditional values often clash with modern human rights ideals, the role of media becomes especially significant.    This section explores the strategies employed by activists, the challenges they face, and the broader implications of their engagement.

### The Importance of Media Engagement

Media serves as a powerful tool for shaping public perception and influencing political discourse. LGBTQ activists in Myanmar recognize that by engaging with various media outlets, they can raise awareness about the challenges faced by the community. This engagement includes traditional media, such as newspapers and television, as well as digital platforms, including social media and blogs.

**Creating Visibility**    Visibility is a double-edged sword for LGBTQ activists. While increased visibility can foster understanding and acceptance, it also exposes individuals to potential backlash. Activists like Wai Wai Nu have utilized media to share personal stories, highlighting the struggles and triumphs of LGBTQ individuals in Myanmar. By putting a face to the movement, they humanize the issues and challenge stereotypes.

For instance, a documentary featuring the life of an LGBTQ activist in Myanmar can significantly impact public sentiment. Such narratives can evoke empathy and encourage discussions around acceptance and equality. However, it is essential to navigate the media landscape carefully, as sensationalism can lead to misrepresentation.

## Political Engagement and Advocacy

In addition to media engagement, political advocacy is vital for driving legislative change. LGBTQ activists in Myanmar have worked to engage political leaders and influence policy decisions. This involves direct lobbying, participation in public forums, and collaboration with human rights organizations to advocate for legal reforms.

**Building Alliances** Forming alliances with sympathetic political figures can enhance the effectiveness of advocacy efforts. For example, collaborating with progressive lawmakers can lead to the introduction of bills aimed at decriminalizing homosexuality or protecting LGBTQ rights. Activists often participate in meetings with these leaders to share their experiences and provide data on the impacts of discrimination.

**Challenges in Political Engagement** Despite the potential for positive change, engaging with politics in Myanmar is fraught with challenges. Activists often face hostility from conservative factions within the government and society. The legal framework remains largely unfavorable, with laws criminalizing same-sex relationships still in place. This creates a precarious environment for activists, who must balance their advocacy with personal safety.

## Utilizing Social Media

In the digital age, social media has emerged as a critical platform for LGBTQ activism. Platforms like Facebook, Twitter, and Instagram allow activists to disseminate information quickly and reach a broader audience. Social media campaigns can mobilize support, organize events, and create a sense of community among LGBTQ individuals.

**Case Study: #LoveIsLove Campaign** One notable example is the #LoveIsLove campaign, which gained traction on social media in Myanmar. This campaign encouraged individuals to share their love stories, regardless of sexual orientation, using the hashtag to foster solidarity and visibility. The campaign not only celebrated love but also challenged societal norms, promoting a message of acceptance and equality.

## Media Representation and Responsibility

As LGBTQ activists engage with media, they must also consider the ethical implications of representation. It is crucial to portray LGBTQ individuals authentically and avoid perpetuating harmful stereotypes. Activists advocate for responsible media practices that highlight diversity within the community, including different sexual orientations, gender identities, and cultural backgrounds.

**The Role of Journalists** Journalists play a pivotal role in shaping narratives around LGBTQ issues. Activists often collaborate with journalists to ensure accurate reporting and to provide context for stories. Training sessions for journalists on LGBTQ issues can help reduce biases and foster a more inclusive media landscape.

## Conclusion

Engaging with media and politics is an essential component of LGBTQ activism in Myanmar. By leveraging media platforms and building political alliances, activists can amplify their voices and advocate for meaningful change. However, they must navigate a complex landscape filled with challenges, including societal prejudices and legal barriers. As the movement continues to evolve, the importance of visibility, responsible representation, and strategic political engagement will remain paramount in the fight for LGBTQ rights in Myanmar.

## Lobbying for Legal Reforms

Lobbying for legal reforms is a critical component of the LGBTQ rights movement in Myanmar. This process involves advocating for changes to existing laws and the creation of new legislation that protects the rights of LGBTQ individuals. The need for legal reform is underscored by the criminalization of homosexuality in Myanmar, where Section 377 of the Penal Code remains a significant barrier to equality and justice.

## Understanding the Legal Landscape

The legal framework surrounding LGBTQ rights in Myanmar is complex and deeply rooted in historical, cultural, and religious contexts. Section 377, inherited from British colonial law, criminalizes "unnatural offenses," which has been used to target and persecute LGBTQ individuals. This law not only fosters discrimination but also perpetuates a culture of fear and stigma.

## Challenges in Lobbying

Lobbying for legal reforms in Myanmar presents several challenges:

+ **Cultural Resistance:** Traditional beliefs and societal norms often oppose LGBTQ rights, making it difficult to garner public support for legal changes.

+ **Political Climate:** Myanmar's political landscape is fraught with instability, and the government may prioritize other issues over LGBTQ rights, viewing them as controversial.

+ **Limited Resources:** Many LGBTQ advocacy groups operate on limited budgets and face challenges in mobilizing sufficient resources for effective lobbying.

## Strategies for Effective Lobbying

To overcome these challenges, activists have employed various strategies:

+ **Building Coalitions:** Forming alliances with human rights organizations, legal experts, and sympathetic political figures can amplify the call for reform.

+ **Public Awareness Campaigns:** Educating the public about LGBTQ issues and the need for legal reforms can help shift societal attitudes. Campaigns utilizing social media, workshops, and community events have proven effective.

+ **Engagement with Policymakers:** Direct engagement with lawmakers through meetings, petitions, and public forums can create pressure for change. Providing lawmakers with data and personal testimonies can humanize the issues at stake.

## Successful Examples of Lobbying Efforts

Several successful lobbying efforts highlight the potential for change:

+ **The Decriminalization Movement in India:** The successful repeal of Section 377 in India in 2018 serves as an inspiring example for LGBTQ activists in Myanmar. This victory was achieved through years of advocacy, legal challenges, and public support.

+ **Collaborative Advocacy:** In Myanmar, collaboration with international NGOs has helped amplify local voices. Organizations like Human Rights Watch and Amnesty International have provided resources and visibility to local campaigns.

## The Role of International Support

International support plays a crucial role in lobbying for legal reforms. Global LGBTQ organizations can offer technical assistance, funding, and a platform for activists to share their stories. Engaging with international human rights bodies, such as the United Nations, can also elevate the urgency of the cause and put pressure on the Myanmar government to comply with international human rights standards.

## Future Aspirations

The path to legal reform is fraught with obstacles, yet the aspirations of LGBTQ activists in Myanmar remain steadfast. Continued advocacy for the repeal of discriminatory laws, the establishment of anti-discrimination protections, and the promotion of LGBTQ-inclusive policies are essential for achieving equality. As the movement evolves, the hope is to foster a society where LGBTQ individuals can live openly and freely, without fear of persecution.

In conclusion, lobbying for legal reforms is a vital aspect of the LGBTQ rights movement in Myanmar. By understanding the legal landscape, overcoming challenges, employing effective strategies, and leveraging international support, activists can pave the way for meaningful change. The journey toward equality is ongoing, but with determination and solidarity, the vision of a just and inclusive society can become a reality.

## Initiating Change at the Grassroots Level

Grassroots activism represents a powerful mechanism for social change, particularly in contexts where systemic barriers impede progress. In Myanmar, where LGBTQ rights have historically been marginalized, grassroots initiatives have become essential for fostering community engagement, raising awareness, and advocating for policy reform. This section explores the theoretical underpinnings of grassroots activism, identifies the challenges faced by LGBTQ movements in Myanmar, and highlights successful examples of grassroots initiatives that have catalyzed change.

## Theoretical Framework

Grassroots activism is often rooted in the principles of social movement theory, which emphasizes the role of collective action in challenging societal norms and injustices. According to Tilly and Tarrow (2007), social movements emerge from the interactions between political opportunities, mobilizing structures, and framing processes. In the context of LGBTQ activism in Myanmar, grassroots efforts can be understood through the lens of these three components:

+ **Political Opportunities:** The political landscape in Myanmar has been characterized by fluctuating levels of repression and openness. Activists must navigate these dynamics to identify windows of opportunity for mobilization.

+ **Mobilizing Structures:** Grassroots organizations often rely on informal networks, community groups, and social media platforms to mobilize supporters and disseminate information.

+ **Framing Processes:** Effective grassroots movements frame their messages in ways that resonate with broader societal values, such as human rights, equality, and justice.

## Challenges Faced by LGBTQ Grassroots Movements

Despite the potential for grassroots activism to effect change, LGBTQ activists in Myanmar encounter numerous obstacles:

+ **Cultural Stigmatization:** Deep-rooted prejudices against LGBTQ individuals often hinder open discussions about sexual orientation and gender identity. Activists must confront societal norms that stigmatize queerness while promoting acceptance.

+ **Legal Barriers:** The criminalization of homosexuality under Section 377 of the Penal Code poses significant risks for activists. Legal repercussions can deter individuals from participating in advocacy efforts.

+ **Limited Resources:** Grassroots organizations often operate with minimal funding and resources, making it challenging to sustain long-term initiatives and outreach programs.

+ **Safety Concerns:** Activists face threats of violence, harassment, and surveillance. Ensuring the safety of participants is paramount, yet difficult to achieve in a hostile environment.

## Successful Examples of Grassroots Initiatives

Despite these challenges, several grassroots initiatives have successfully initiated change in Myanmar:

- **Community-Based Workshops:** Organizations such as the *Yangon Pride Network* have conducted workshops aimed at educating LGBTQ individuals about their rights and providing skills for activism. These workshops foster a sense of community and empower participants to advocate for change.

- **Social Media Campaigns:** Activists have utilized platforms like Facebook and Instagram to raise awareness about LGBTQ issues, share personal stories, and mobilize support for events such as pride marches. The *#LoveIsLove* campaign gained significant traction, promoting messages of love and acceptance across Myanmar.

- **Collaborative Events:** Grassroots organizations often collaborate with allies in the broader human rights community to organize events that celebrate LGBTQ identities while advocating for legal reforms. For instance, the annual *Yangon Pride Festival* has become a platform for visibility and solidarity, attracting participants from various backgrounds.

- **Health and Support Services:** Initiatives like the *Rainbow Health Network* provide essential health services to LGBTQ individuals, addressing unique health needs and promoting inclusive healthcare practices. These services not only improve health outcomes but also build trust within the community.

## Conclusion

Initiating change at the grassroots level is vital for advancing LGBTQ rights in Myanmar. By leveraging community support, addressing societal stigma, and advocating for legal reforms, grassroots activists can create a more inclusive environment for LGBTQ individuals. The resilience and determination of these activists serve as a testament to the power of collective action in the face of adversity. As grassroots movements continue to evolve, they hold the potential to inspire broader societal change and pave the way for a more equitable future for all.

# Bibliography

[1]  Tilly, C., & Tarrow, S. (2007). *Contentious performances*. Cambridge University Press.

## Collaborating with International LGBTQ Organizations

In the quest for LGBTQ rights in Myanmar, collaboration with international LGBTQ organizations has emerged as a pivotal strategy for amplifying local voices, securing resources, and fostering a global network of support. This section explores the significance of these collaborations, the challenges faced, and the successes achieved through strategic partnerships.

### The Importance of International Collaboration

International LGBTQ organizations play a crucial role in providing resources, advocacy tools, and visibility to local movements. By partnering with these organizations, activists in Myanmar can access a wealth of knowledge and experience from global LGBTQ struggles. For instance, organizations such as ILGA (International Lesbian, Gay, Bisexual, Trans and Intersex Association) and OutRight Action International have extensive networks that can help amplify the voices of Myanmar's LGBTQ community on a global stage.

Moreover, these collaborations facilitate the sharing of best practices in activism. For example, the experience of LGBTQ activists in countries with more progressive policies can offer valuable insights into effective advocacy strategies, campaign planning, and community organizing. This exchange of knowledge is crucial in shaping a robust LGBTQ rights movement in Myanmar, where activists often face significant challenges due to a conservative societal backdrop.

## Challenges in Collaboration

Despite the benefits, collaborating with international organizations is not without its challenges.   One of the primary concerns is the potential for cultural misunderstandings.   International organizations may not fully grasp the local context, leading to initiatives that, while well-intentioned, may not resonate with the unique challenges faced by Myanmar's LGBTQ community.   For instance, campaigns that work in Western contexts might not be effective in Myanmar due to differing cultural norms and societal expectations.

Additionally, there is the risk of dependency on international funding and support.   While financial assistance is critical for grassroots movements, over-reliance on external funding can undermine local autonomy and sustainability.   Activists must navigate the delicate balance between accepting necessary support and maintaining their independence to advocate for their community's needs authentically.

## Successful Collaborations: Case Studies

Several successful collaborations illustrate the potential of international partnerships in advancing LGBTQ rights in Myanmar. One notable example is the partnership between local activists and international organizations during the 2019 Pride Month celebrations in Yangon.   This event, which aimed to raise awareness and promote acceptance, was supported by various international LGBTQ organizations that provided funding, resources, and visibility.   The collaboration not only brought attention to the LGBTQ community in Myanmar but also fostered a sense of solidarity and empowerment among local activists.

Another significant collaboration occurred in the realm of legal advocacy. Myanmar's LGBTQ activists worked alongside international human rights organizations to challenge discriminatory laws. Through coordinated efforts, they were able to present a compelling case to legal bodies, highlighting the need for reform in existing laws that criminalize homosexuality. This collaboration not only strengthened the legal arguments but also brought international attention to the issue, thereby increasing pressure on the Myanmar government to consider legal reforms.

## Building a Global Network of Support

The collaboration with international LGBTQ organizations is not merely about immediate gains; it is also about building a sustainable global network of support. By engaging with international allies, Myanmar's LGBTQ activists can create a platform for ongoing dialogue and exchange. This network can serve as a lifeline during crises, providing resources, legal assistance, and solidarity when local conditions become hostile.

Furthermore, these collaborations can aid in the dissemination of information regarding the plight of LGBTQ individuals in Myanmar. By leveraging international media channels, activists can bring global attention to local issues, thereby fostering a sense of accountability among policymakers. The global LGBTQ community's solidarity can create a powerful force for change, as demonstrated during the international campaigns against human rights violations in Myanmar.

## Conclusion

In conclusion, the collaboration with international LGBTQ organizations is a vital component of the movement for LGBTQ rights in Myanmar. While challenges exist, the potential benefits—ranging from resource access to global visibility—are significant. By strategically engaging with international allies, Myanmar's LGBTQ activists can enhance their advocacy efforts, navigate cultural complexities, and build a resilient movement capable of effecting real change. The future of LGBTQ rights in Myanmar hinges on these collaborations, as they foster not only local empowerment but also a global commitment to equality and justice for all.

# The Challenges and Dangers of Activism

## Threats and Harassment

In the landscape of LGBTQ activism in Myanmar, one of the most pressing issues faced by advocates like Wai Wai Nu is the omnipresent threat of harassment. This section delves into the various forms of threats and harassment that LGBTQ activists encounter, examining the implications of these experiences on their work, mental health, and personal lives.

## Understanding Threats and Harassment

The threats faced by LGBTQ activists can be categorized into several forms: verbal harassment, physical violence, social ostracism, and institutional discrimination. Each of these categories represents a layer of risk that activists must navigate daily.

**Verbal Harassment**   Verbal harassment often manifests in the form of hate speech, derogatory comments, and public shaming.  Such harassment is not only demoralizing but can also lead to a chilling effect, where individuals feel discouraged from expressing their identities or advocating for their rights.  For instance, activists in Myanmar have reported instances where they were publicly ridiculed during community events or on social media platforms, creating an environment of fear and isolation.

**Physical Violence**   Physical violence represents a more severe threat. Reports of assaults against LGBTQ individuals, including activists, have surfaced, highlighting the dangers associated with standing up for one's rights in a conservative society.  For example, there have been documented cases of activists being attacked during pride events or community gatherings, leading to injuries and, in some cases, severe trauma. This violence is often exacerbated by the lack of legal protections for LGBTQ individuals, which emboldens perpetrators and leaves victims with little recourse.

**Social Ostracism**   Social ostracism can be equally damaging. Activists may find themselves alienated from their families, friends, and communities due to their advocacy work.   This social isolation can lead to significant mental health challenges, as individuals grapple with feelings of abandonment and rejection. The pressure to conform to traditional societal norms often forces activists to choose between their identities and their relationships, creating an internal conflict that can be deeply distressing.

**Institutional Discrimination**   Institutional discrimination further complicates the situation for LGBTQ activists. Laws that criminalize homosexuality and other forms of sexual expression create an environment where activists are constantly at risk of legal repercussions. This legal framework not only legitimizes harassment but also discourages individuals from seeking help or reporting incidents of violence.  For example, a study conducted by the International Lesbian, Gay, Bisexual, Trans and Intersex Association (ILGA) indicated that many LGBTQ individuals in Myanmar are reluctant to approach law enforcement due to fear of further victimization.

## The Psychological Impact of Threats and Harassment

The psychological toll of living under the threat of harassment cannot be overstated. Activists often experience heightened levels of anxiety, depression, and post-traumatic stress disorder (PTSD) as a result of their experiences. The constant vigilance required to navigate a hostile environment can lead to burnout and a sense of hopelessness.

Research indicates that individuals who face chronic stress due to discrimination and violence are at a higher risk for various mental health issues. For example, a 2018 study published in the *Journal of Homosexuality* found that LGBTQ individuals in oppressive environments reported significantly higher rates of anxiety and depressive disorders compared to their heterosexual counterparts. This highlights the urgent need for mental health support tailored specifically for LGBTQ activists.

## Coping Mechanisms and Resilience

Despite these challenges, many activists develop coping mechanisms to manage the stress and trauma associated with threats and harassment. Building supportive networks with fellow activists can provide a sense of community and belonging, which is crucial for mental well-being. Additionally, engaging in self-care practices, such as mindfulness and therapy, can help individuals process their experiences and foster resilience.

One notable example is the establishment of peer support groups within the LGBTQ community in Myanmar. These groups offer safe spaces for individuals to share their experiences, seek advice, and provide emotional support to one another. Such initiatives not only empower activists but also create a collective strength that can be harnessed in the fight for LGBTQ rights.

## Conclusion

In conclusion, threats and harassment are pervasive issues that significantly impact LGBTQ activists in Myanmar. Understanding the various forms of these threats, their psychological impact, and the coping mechanisms employed by activists is essential for addressing the challenges they face. As the movement for LGBTQ rights continues to grow, it is imperative that both local and international communities recognize these issues and work collaboratively to create a safer environment for activists and the LGBTQ community at large.

$$\text{Mental Health Impact} = f(\text{Threats, Harassment, Social Support}) \qquad (13)$$

This equation illustrates the relationship between the threats and harassment faced by LGBTQ activists and their mental health outcomes, emphasizing the critical role of social support in mitigating negative effects.

## Facing Legal Consequences

In Myanmar, the legal landscape for LGBTQ individuals is fraught with challenges and dangers. The existence of laws that criminalize homosexuality creates an environment where LGBTQ activists, like Wai Wai Nu, face significant legal repercussions for their advocacy. This section explores the legal consequences faced by activists, the implications of these laws, and the broader impact on the LGBTQ community.

## Criminalization of Homosexuality

Myanmar's Penal Code, particularly Section 377, criminalizes same-sex sexual conduct. This law, which dates back to British colonial rule, not only targets individuals but also serves as a tool for oppression against the LGBTQ community. The existence of such laws fosters a culture of fear, where individuals are reluctant to express their sexual orientation or gender identity openly. The legal ramifications of being accused of homosexuality can include imprisonment, fines, and societal ostracism.

For instance, in 2017, a prominent LGBTQ activist was arrested under this law during a raid on a safe space for LGBTQ individuals in Yangon. The legal charges brought against them were not merely punitive; they were intended to send a message to the community about the risks associated with activism. This incident exemplifies the potential consequences that LGBTQ activists face in Myanmar, where the law is weaponized against them.

## Legal Repercussions for Activism

Activism in support of LGBTQ rights often places individuals at risk of legal action. Engaging in protests, organizing community events, or even speaking out against discriminatory laws can lead to harassment by law enforcement. Activists may find themselves facing charges that are unrelated to their advocacy but are instead used as a means to silence dissent.

One notable example is the case of a grassroots organization that organized a pride event in Yangon. The event was met with police intervention, and several organizers were detained. They faced charges of public indecency and incitement, illustrating how the legal system can be manipulated to suppress activism. The fear of arrest and legal consequences can deter individuals from participating in movements for change, stifling the growth of the LGBTQ rights movement in Myanmar.

## The Role of Legal Defense

Given the potential legal consequences of activism, many LGBTQ activists seek legal representation to navigate the complexities of the law. Human rights organizations often provide legal aid to those facing charges, helping to challenge unjust laws and advocate for the rights of the accused. However, the availability of legal resources is limited, and not all activists have access to adequate legal representation.

The case of Wai Wai Nu is illustrative. After facing threats of legal action for her activism, she sought the assistance of a human rights lawyer who specialized in LGBTQ issues. Together, they worked to challenge the charges brought against her, arguing that the laws were discriminatory and violated her rights. This legal battle highlighted the importance of having knowledgeable legal allies in the fight against unjust laws.

## Public Scrutiny and Legal Consequences

Activists also face the pressure of public scrutiny, which can exacerbate the legal consequences they encounter. Media coverage of LGBTQ issues in Myanmar is often sensationalized, leading to public backlash against activists. This scrutiny can result in increased surveillance by authorities and a heightened risk of arrest.

For example, when Wai Wai Nu publicly spoke out against the legal discrimination faced by LGBTQ individuals, she became a target for both the media and law enforcement. The negative portrayal of her activism in the press contributed to a climate of fear, where her actions were met with hostility rather than support. This environment not only affects individual activists but also discourages broader participation in the movement.

## Mental Health Implications

The legal consequences of activism can also take a toll on the mental health of LGBTQ individuals. The constant threat of arrest, coupled with societal stigma, can lead to anxiety, depression, and feelings of isolation. Activists often grapple with the dual burden of fighting for their rights while managing the psychological impact of their activism.

Wai Wai Nu has spoken candidly about the mental health challenges she faced during her activism. The stress of potential legal repercussions weighed heavily on her, impacting her ability to engage fully in her work. This highlights the need for mental health support within the LGBTQ community, particularly for those on the front lines of activism.

## Conclusion

Facing legal consequences is an ever-present reality for LGBTQ activists in Myanmar. The criminalization of homosexuality, coupled with the risks associated with activism, creates a challenging environment for those advocating for change. Legal repercussions can hinder the progress of the LGBTQ rights movement, as fear of arrest and public scrutiny deter participation. As activists like Wai Wai Nu continue to fight for their rights, the importance of legal support, mental health resources, and public awareness becomes increasingly critical in overcoming these challenges. The journey toward equality and acceptance in Myanmar is fraught with obstacles, but the resilience of activists shines through in their unwavering commitment to justice.

## The Pressure of Public Scrutiny

The journey of an activist is often fraught with challenges, and one of the most significant hurdles faced by Wai Wai Nu was the intense pressure of public scrutiny. In a society where traditional values are deeply entrenched, any deviation from the norm can attract unwanted attention and criticism. This scrutiny can manifest in various forms, from social media backlash to public protests, and it can have profound implications for both personal and professional life.

Public scrutiny can be understood through the lens of Goffman's *Presentation of Self in Everyday Life*, where he posits that individuals perform roles based on societal expectations. For activists like Wai Wai Nu, the pressure to maintain a certain public persona can be overwhelming. The expectation to embody the ideals of the LGBTQ rights movement while navigating the complexities of cultural and societal norms creates a dichotomy that can lead to significant stress.

$$P = \frac{S}{E} \tag{14}$$

Where $P$ represents the pressure of public scrutiny, $S$ is the level of societal expectations, and $E$ is the individual's ability to manage those expectations. As societal expectations rise, the pressure experienced by activists can become increasingly difficult to manage, leading to potential burnout and mental health challenges.

Wai Wai Nu faced this pressure head-on as she became a visible figure in the fight for LGBTQ rights in Myanmar. The media often portrayed her as a representative of the entire LGBTQ community, which placed an immense burden on her shoulders. This phenomenon is known as *representational burden*, where individuals from marginalized groups are expected to speak for and represent their entire community, a role that can be both empowering and exhausting.

The pressure of public scrutiny can lead to several problems, including:

+ **Mental Health Struggles:** The constant evaluation by the public can lead to anxiety, depression, and other mental health issues. Activists may feel isolated, fearing that their voices will be misrepresented or that they will be attacked for their beliefs.

+ **Self-Censorship:** In an effort to avoid backlash, activists may feel compelled to censor their opinions or dilute their messages. This self-censorship can hinder the effectiveness of their advocacy and limit their ability to express their true selves.

+ **Impact on Personal Relationships:** The scrutiny can extend beyond the activist's public life and seep into their personal relationships. Friends and family may feel the pressure as well, leading to strained relationships and a sense of isolation.

For example, during a high-profile campaign advocating for LGBTQ rights, Wai Wai Nu found herself at the center of a media storm. While her efforts garnered support from progressive factions, they also attracted criticism from conservative groups. This duality of support and opposition exemplifies the challenges faced by activists in the public eye. The backlash often included derogatory comments on social media and public statements from influential figures questioning her motives and integrity.

Moreover, the pressure of public scrutiny often forces activists to engage in a continuous cycle of self-presentation and management. They must navigate the fine line between authenticity and the expectations imposed upon them by society. This balancing act can lead to a phenomenon known as *impression management*, where individuals consciously attempt to influence the perceptions of others.

In Wai Wai Nu's case, she utilized various platforms to share her story and advocate for change, yet she remained acutely aware of the potential repercussions of her visibility. This awareness often required her to engage in strategic communication, carefully crafting her messages to resonate with diverse audiences while remaining true to her values.

The pressure of public scrutiny is further compounded by the intersectionality of identity. For Wai Wai Nu, being a woman and an LGBTQ activist in Myanmar adds layers of complexity to her public persona. The societal expectations placed upon her as a woman often clash with her role as an activist, creating a unique set of challenges that she must navigate daily.

In conclusion, the pressure of public scrutiny is an inescapable reality for activists like Wai Wai Nu. It shapes their experiences, influences their actions, and impacts their mental health. Understanding this pressure is crucial for fostering a supportive environment for activists, allowing them to thrive in their advocacy while maintaining their well-being. As the LGBTQ rights movement in Myanmar continues to evolve, it is essential to recognize and address the challenges posed by public scrutiny, ensuring that activists can continue their vital work without the weight of societal expectations stifling their voices.

## Balancing Personal and Activist Life

The journey of an activist is often marked by a profound commitment to a cause that transcends personal boundaries. For Wai Wai Nu, balancing the demands of activism with personal life has been a complex and challenging endeavor. The interplay between these two spheres can lead to significant emotional and psychological stress, as well as potential conflicts in relationships.

### The Theory of Work-Life Balance

Work-life balance is a concept that has garnered attention across various fields, including psychology, sociology, and organizational behavior. It refers to the equilibrium between the time and energy devoted to work (or activism, in this context) and that allocated to personal life. Theories such as the *Role Theory* posit that individuals occupy multiple roles—such as activist, friend, partner, and family member—each with its own set of expectations and responsibilities. The challenge lies in managing these roles without allowing one to overshadow the others.

### Challenges Faced by Activists

Activists like Wai Wai Nu often face unique challenges when attempting to maintain this balance:

+ **Time Management:** The demands of activism can be overwhelming, often requiring long hours of organizing events, attending meetings, and engaging with the community. This can lead to neglect of personal relationships and self-care. For instance, Wai Wai recalls instances where she missed family gatherings and social events due to her commitment to LGBTQ rights advocacy.

+ **Emotional Exhaustion:** The emotional toll of fighting against systemic discrimination can lead to burnout. Activists frequently encounter resistance, hostility, and even threats, which can weigh heavily on mental health. Studies indicate that burnout is prevalent among activists, with symptoms including fatigue, cynicism, and reduced efficacy.

+ **Social Isolation:** The intense focus on activism can lead to feelings of isolation. As activists become more engrossed in their work, they may inadvertently distance themselves from friends and family who do not share the same level of commitment or understanding. Wai Wai has experienced this firsthand, feeling that her friends could not relate to the struggles she faced in her advocacy work.

+ **Identity Conflict:** Navigating multiple identities—such as being a queer individual and an activist—can create internal conflict. This duality may lead to feelings of inadequacy or guilt when one role takes precedence over the other. For example, Wai Wai has grappled with the pressure to be a "perfect" activist while also wanting to embrace her personal life fully.

## Strategies for Balance

Despite these challenges, Wai Wai has developed strategies to create a more sustainable balance between her personal and activist life:

+ **Setting Boundaries:** Establishing clear boundaries between activism and personal time is crucial. Wai Wai learned to designate specific hours for activism and to prioritize personal commitments. This practice not only helps in managing time effectively but also ensures that her relationships do not suffer.

+ **Self-Care Practices:** Engaging in self-care is essential for maintaining mental health. Wai Wai incorporates activities such as meditation, exercise, and spending time with loved ones into her routine. Research shows that self-care can enhance resilience and improve overall well-being, allowing activists to recharge and return to their work with renewed energy.

+ **Building a Support Network:** Connecting with other activists who understand the struggles of balancing personal and activist life can provide emotional support. Wai Wai has found solace in forming friendships with fellow activists, creating a community that shares both the burdens and joys of their work. This network serves as a source of encouragement and understanding.

+ **Engaging in Open Communication:** Maintaining open lines of communication with friends and family about the demands of activism can foster understanding and support. Wai Wai emphasizes the importance of sharing her experiences with loved ones, which helps them comprehend her commitment and the challenges she faces.

## Real-Life Examples

Wai Wai's journey exemplifies the ongoing struggle for balance. One poignant example occurred during a significant LGBTQ event in Myanmar. While she was deeply involved in organizing the event, her partner expressed feelings of neglect, leading to a heartfelt conversation about their needs and expectations. This moment prompted Wai Wai to reassess her priorities and implement more structured time for their relationship amidst her activism.

Another instance involved a mental health workshop that Wai Wai organized, which was designed not only for the community but also for activists themselves. This initiative aimed to address the unique stressors faced by LGBTQ activists, highlighting the importance of mental well-being in sustaining activism.

In conclusion, balancing personal and activist life is an ongoing challenge for many, including Wai Wai Nu. By employing strategies such as setting boundaries, practicing self-care, building support networks, and engaging in open communication, activists can create a more harmonious existence. The lessons learned from these experiences not only contribute to personal growth but also enhance the effectiveness of their advocacy efforts, ultimately fostering a more resilient and empowered LGBTQ rights movement in Myanmar.

## Standing Strong Against Adversities

In the face of adversity, resilience becomes a crucial pillar for activists like Wai Wai Nu. The journey of advocating for LGBTQ rights in Myanmar is fraught with challenges, ranging from societal discrimination to legal repercussions. This section explores the multifaceted nature of these adversities and the strategies employed to overcome them.

## Understanding Adversity

Adversity can be defined as a state of hardship or misfortune that tests an individual's resolve. In the context of LGBTQ activism in Myanmar, this adversity manifests in various forms, including social ostracism, threats of violence, and systemic legal discrimination. The psychological impact of these adversities can be profound, often leading to feelings of isolation and despair among activists.

## Theoretical Framework

To comprehend the resilience exhibited by activists, we can draw upon the theory of psychological resilience. According to [?], resilience is not merely an individual trait but a dynamic process that involves positive adaptation in the face of adversity. This process can be influenced by various factors, including social support, community engagement, and personal beliefs.

The equation for resilience can be expressed as:

$$R = (S + C + P) \times E$$

Where: - $R$ is resilience, - $S$ is social support, - $C$ is community involvement, - $P$ is personal strength, - $E$ is external environment.

In the case of Wai Wai Nu, her resilience is bolstered by a strong network of allies, a deep commitment to her cause, and the supportive environment she cultivates within her community.

## Facing Societal Discrimination

Wai Wai Nu's journey began in a society where traditional norms often clash with the realities of LGBTQ existence. Discrimination is prevalent in many aspects of life, from employment opportunities to family acceptance. For instance, many LGBTQ individuals face rejection from their families, leading to a loss of emotional and financial support.

Wai Wai's experience with societal discrimination is not unique. According to a report by [?], 75% of LGBTQ individuals in Myanmar have experienced some form of discrimination, highlighting the urgent need for advocacy and change.

To combat these societal challenges, Wai Wai employs a strategy of visibility and education. By sharing her story and the stories of others, she humanizes the LGBTQ experience, fostering empathy and understanding within the broader community.

## Legal Repercussions

Legal challenges pose another significant hurdle for LGBTQ activists in Myanmar. The country's colonial-era laws criminalize homosexuality, leading to arrests and harassment of LGBTQ individuals. This legal framework creates a climate of fear that can stifle activism.

Wai Wai Nu faced these legal adversities head-on. In 2015, she was part of a landmark case that challenged the constitutionality of anti-LGBTQ laws. Although the case did not result in immediate legal reform, it set a precedent for future challenges and galvanized the LGBTQ community to continue their fight for justice.

The legal landscape can be represented as follows:

$$L = \frac{D}{R}$$

Where: - $L$ is the likelihood of legal repercussions, - $D$ is the degree of activism, - $R$ is the resilience of the community.

As activism increases, so does the potential for legal repercussions; however, as resilience strengthens, the community becomes better equipped to face these challenges.

## Mental Health Challenges

The mental health of activists is often compromised due to the stresses of their work. The constant threat of violence, coupled with societal rejection, can lead to anxiety, depression, and burnout.

Wai Wai Nu emphasizes the importance of mental health support within the activist community. She advocates for the establishment of peer support groups where activists can share their experiences and coping strategies. This approach not only fosters a sense of belonging but also reinforces the collective strength of the community.

Research by [?] shows that community support can significantly mitigate the adverse effects of discrimination on mental health, reinforcing the idea that standing strong against adversities is often a communal effort.

## Building Solidarity

One of the most effective strategies Wai Wai employs is building solidarity among different marginalized groups. By uniting LGBTQ rights with other social justice movements, such as women's rights and ethnic minority rights, she broadens the base of support and creates a more formidable front against oppression.

An example of this solidarity in action was the 2019 Pride Parade in Yangon, where LGBTQ activists marched alongside women's rights advocates and ethnic minority representatives. This collective action not only showcased the intersectionality of their struggles but also amplified their voices in the fight for equality.

## Conclusion

Standing strong against adversities requires a multifaceted approach that combines resilience, community support, and strategic activism. Wai Wai Nu's journey illustrates that while the challenges are significant, the strength found in solidarity and the unwavering commitment to justice can pave the way for meaningful change. As she continues her advocacy, she embodies the belief that adversity can be transformed into a catalyst for empowerment, inspiring others to join the fight for LGBTQ rights in Myanmar and beyond.

## Supporting Fellow Activists

In the landscape of LGBTQ activism, the act of supporting fellow activists is not only a moral imperative but also a strategic necessity. Activism thrives in a community where individuals uplift one another, share resources, and build networks of solidarity. This section explores the importance of mutual support among activists, the challenges they face, and the various ways in which they can foster an environment of collaboration and resilience.

## The Importance of Mutual Support

The foundation of any successful movement lies in its ability to cultivate a sense of community among its members. According to social movement theory, collective identity is crucial for mobilization and sustained activism. When activists see themselves as part of a larger community, they are more likely to engage in collective actions and support one another in times of need. This sense of belonging can counteract feelings of isolation and despair, which are often prevalent in marginalized communities.

## Challenges Faced by Activists

Despite the shared goals of LGBTQ activists, challenges often arise that can hinder collaboration. These include:

+ **Resource Scarcity:** Many activists operate with limited funding and resources, which can lead to competition rather than collaboration.

+ **Burnout:** The emotional toll of activism can lead to burnout, making it difficult for individuals to support their peers.

+ **Differences in Priorities:** Activists may have varying priorities based on their personal experiences, leading to conflict within the community.

To address these challenges, it is essential for activists to create systems of support that prioritize mental health and resource sharing.

## Building Networks of Solidarity

One effective way to support fellow activists is through the establishment of networks that facilitate collaboration. These networks can take various forms:

+ **Peer Support Groups:** These groups provide a safe space for activists to share their experiences, discuss challenges, and offer emotional support. Regular meetings can help in building trust and solidarity.

+ **Resource Sharing Platforms:** Online platforms can be created to share resources such as funding opportunities, educational materials, and legal assistance. This approach can mitigate resource scarcity and foster collaboration.

+ **Skill-Sharing Workshops:** Hosting workshops where activists can share their skills—whether in media training, public speaking, or legal advocacy—can enhance the overall capacity of the movement.

## Examples of Support in Action

There are numerous examples of successful activist networks that have provided essential support to their members:

+ **The Myanmar Queer Film Festival:** This annual event not only showcases LGBTQ films but also serves as a platform for local activists to connect, share their stories, and collaborate on future projects.

- **The Rainbow Network:** A coalition of LGBTQ organizations in Myanmar that works together to provide training, resources, and advocacy support. Their collaborative efforts have led to significant legal reforms and increased visibility for LGBTQ issues.

- **Mental Health Initiatives:** Programs that focus on the mental health of activists have been established, recognizing the high levels of stress and trauma associated with activism. These initiatives provide counseling and peer support to help activists cope with the emotional demands of their work.

## The Role of Allyship

Supporting fellow activists also involves recognizing the role of allies. Allies can amplify the voices of marginalized activists, provide resources, and help to create a more inclusive environment. Effective allyship requires:

- **Listening and Learning:** Allies should take the time to understand the experiences and needs of LGBTQ activists and communities.

- **Using Privilege Responsibly:** Allies must leverage their privilege to advocate for change and support those who are more marginalized.

- **Standing in Solidarity:** Allies should actively participate in actions and campaigns led by LGBTQ activists, demonstrating their commitment to the cause.

## Conclusion

Supporting fellow activists is a vital component of building a resilient and effective LGBTQ rights movement. By fostering an environment of mutual aid, sharing resources, and engaging in allyship, activists can navigate the challenges of their work more effectively. As we continue to fight for equality and justice, let us remember that our strength lies in our solidarity, and together, we can create a more inclusive and supportive community for all.

$$\text{Collective Identity} = \sum_{i=1}^{n} \text{Individual Experiences} \tag{15}$$

This equation illustrates that the collective identity of a movement is derived from the individual experiences of its members, emphasizing the importance of supporting one another in the quest for justice.

## Coping with Mental Health Challenges

Mental health is an essential yet often overlooked aspect of activism, particularly in the context of LGBTQ rights in Myanmar. Activists like Wai Wai Nu face unique challenges that can severely impact their mental well-being. This section explores the mental health challenges encountered by LGBTQ activists, the theoretical frameworks surrounding these issues, and practical coping strategies that can be employed.

## Understanding Mental Health Challenges

Activism can be a double-edged sword; while it provides a sense of purpose and community, it can also lead to significant stress and mental health issues. According to the *World Health Organization (WHO)*, mental health is defined as a state of well-being in which individuals realize their own abilities, can cope with the normal stresses of life, can work productively and fruitfully, and are able to contribute to their community. However, LGBTQ activists often experience heightened levels of stress due to societal stigma, discrimination, and the emotional toll of advocating for change.

**Theoretical Frameworks** One useful theoretical lens for understanding the mental health challenges faced by LGBTQ activists is the *Minority Stress Theory*. This theory posits that individuals from marginalized groups experience chronic stress due to their social environment, which can lead to mental health issues such as anxiety, depression, and post-traumatic stress disorder (PTSD). The following equation summarizes the relationship between minority stress and mental health outcomes:

$$M = S + E + C \tag{16}$$

where $M$ represents mental health outcomes, $S$ is the stressors related to being part of a minority group, $E$ is the environmental factors contributing to stress, and $C$ is the coping resources available to the individual.

## Common Mental Health Issues

Activists may face various mental health challenges, including:

- **Anxiety Disorders:** The constant threat of violence, discrimination, and social ostracization can lead to chronic anxiety. Activists may feel overwhelmed by the pressure to perform and represent their communities.

+ **Depression:** The emotional burden of activism, coupled with societal rejection, can lead to feelings of hopelessness and despair. This is exacerbated by the lack of support systems in conservative societies.

+ **Burnout:** The relentless nature of activism can lead to physical and emotional exhaustion, often resulting in burnout. Activists may feel that their efforts are futile, leading to disengagement.

+ **Post-Traumatic Stress Disorder (PTSD):** Exposure to violence or harassment can lead to PTSD, characterized by intrusive thoughts, flashbacks, and severe anxiety.

## Coping Strategies

Given the mental health challenges faced by LGBTQ activists, it is crucial to develop effective coping strategies. Here are several approaches that can help:

**Building a Support Network** Creating a strong support network is vital for mental well-being. Activists should seek out friends, family, and fellow activists who understand their experiences. Engaging with local and international LGBTQ organizations can also provide a sense of community and belonging.

**Practicing Self-Care** Self-care is essential for maintaining mental health. Activists should prioritize activities that promote relaxation and joy, such as:

+ **Mindfulness and Meditation:** These practices can help reduce anxiety and improve emotional regulation. Studies have shown that mindfulness can decrease stress levels and enhance overall well-being.

+ **Physical Activity:** Regular exercise has been proven to alleviate symptoms of depression and anxiety. Activities like yoga, running, or dancing can serve as effective outlets for stress.

+ **Creative Expression:** Engaging in creative activities such as art, writing, or music can provide a therapeutic outlet for emotions and experiences.

**Seeking Professional Help** Accessing mental health resources is crucial for those struggling with severe mental health issues. Activists should not hesitate to seek professional help when needed. This may include:

+ **Therapy or Counseling:** Working with a mental health professional can provide coping strategies tailored to individual needs. Cognitive Behavioral Therapy (CBT) has been shown to be particularly effective for anxiety and depression.

+ **Support Groups:** Joining support groups can help individuals connect with others who share similar experiences, fostering a sense of solidarity and understanding.

**Advocating for Mental Health Awareness**    Activists can also play a role in promoting mental health awareness within their communities. By advocating for mental health resources and support systems, they can help reduce stigma and encourage others to seek help.

## Conclusion

Coping with mental health challenges is an integral part of being an LGBTQ activist in Myanmar. By understanding the unique stressors they face and employing effective coping strategies, activists like Wai Wai Nu can not only sustain their mental well-being but also continue their vital work in advocating for LGBTQ rights. As the movement grows, addressing mental health will be crucial in ensuring that activists remain resilient and effective in their fight for equality and acceptance.

## Seeking Protection and Security

In the realm of activism, particularly for marginalized communities such as the LGBTQ population in Myanmar, the quest for protection and security is paramount. Activists like Wai Wai Nu face not only societal discrimination but also direct threats to their safety as they challenge deeply ingrained cultural norms. This section explores the multifaceted aspects of seeking protection and security, highlighting the theoretical frameworks, problems, and real-world examples that illustrate the challenges faced by LGBTQ activists.

### Theoretical Framework

The need for protection and security in activism can be understood through the lens of several theories, including the Theory of Social Movements and the Risk Society Theory. The Theory of Social Movements posits that collective action arises in response to perceived injustices and the need for social change. In this context, LGBTQ activists mobilize to confront systemic discrimination, which inherently places them at risk.

On the other hand, the Risk Society Theory, proposed by Ulrich Beck, emphasizes that modern societies are increasingly characterized by the risks associated with social, political, and environmental changes. LGBTQ activists navigate a landscape fraught with dangers, including physical violence, legal repercussions, and social ostracism. Thus, the quest for protection is not merely a personal concern but a collective necessity for sustaining the movement.

## Identifying Problems

The challenges faced by LGBTQ activists in Myanmar are manifold. Firstly, the legal framework in Myanmar criminalizes homosexuality, creating a hostile environment for activists. The existence of laws that punish same-sex relationships fosters a culture of fear, discouraging individuals from openly advocating for their rights. Activists like Wai Wai Nu have often had to operate in secrecy, aware that their visibility could lead to harassment or arrest.

Moreover, societal attitudes towards LGBTQ individuals are often steeped in prejudice. This societal stigma can manifest in various forms, including workplace discrimination, familial rejection, and violence. Activists seeking protection must navigate these treacherous waters, often relying on informal networks of support and solidarity.

## Examples of Seeking Protection

In practical terms, seeking protection and security has taken various forms for LGBTQ activists in Myanmar. One notable example is the establishment of safe houses and community centers that provide refuge for individuals facing persecution. These safe spaces serve not only as physical shelters but also as hubs for organizing and mobilizing the community.

Additionally, activists have engaged with international human rights organizations to garner support and protection. Collaborations with entities such as Amnesty International and Human Rights Watch have been instrumental in raising awareness of the plight of LGBTQ individuals in Myanmar. These organizations often provide legal assistance, advocacy, and even funding for initiatives aimed at protecting LGBTQ rights.

Furthermore, the use of technology has become a crucial element in the fight for security. Activists have turned to encrypted communication tools to safeguard their identities and coordinate efforts without the risk of surveillance. This technological adaptation reflects a broader trend in contemporary activism, where digital platforms are leveraged for both mobilization and protection.

## Coping Mechanisms

Coping with the inherent dangers of activism requires resilience and strategic planning. Many LGBTQ activists engage in mental health support systems, recognizing the toll that activism can take on their well-being. Group therapy sessions and peer support networks provide safe spaces for individuals to share their experiences and challenges, fostering a sense of community and solidarity.

Moreover, the importance of self-care cannot be overstated. Activists often emphasize the need to balance their activist roles with personal lives, ensuring that they do not become overwhelmed by the pressures of their work. This balance is crucial for sustaining long-term engagement in the movement.

## The Role of International Solidarity

International solidarity plays a vital role in enhancing the security of LGBTQ activists in Myanmar. Global LGBTQ organizations often lend their voices to amplify local struggles, drawing attention to the challenges faced by activists. This external pressure can lead to improved conditions and greater protection for those on the front lines of the fight for rights.

For instance, during international LGBTQ events such as Pride Month, activists from Myanmar have had the opportunity to share their stories and challenges with a global audience. This visibility not only raises awareness but also fosters a sense of interconnectedness among LGBTQ movements worldwide, reinforcing the notion that the struggle for rights is a universal endeavor.

## Conclusion

In conclusion, the pursuit of protection and security for LGBTQ activists in Myanmar is a complex and ongoing battle. It requires a multifaceted approach that encompasses legal advocacy, community support, and international solidarity. As activists like Wai Wai Nu continue to challenge the status quo, the need for safe spaces, mental health resources, and protective measures remains critical. By understanding the theoretical frameworks and real-world challenges associated with seeking protection, we can better appreciate the resilience and courage of those fighting for LGBTQ rights in Myanmar and beyond.

## The Impact on Personal Relationships

The journey of an activist is often fraught with challenges that extend beyond the public sphere, deeply affecting personal relationships. For Wai Wai Nu, the struggle for LGBTQ rights in Myanmar not only demanded immense courage and resilience but also took a toll on her connections with family, friends, and romantic partners. This section explores the multifaceted impact of activism on personal relationships, examining the emotional, social, and psychological dimensions involved.

## Emotional Strain and Isolation

Activism can lead to emotional strain, particularly when one's beliefs and lifestyle diverge significantly from those of family and peers. In traditional societies like Myanmar, where conservative values prevail, coming out as LGBTQ can lead to feelings of isolation. For Wai Wai, the fear of rejection loomed large. The emotional turmoil was compounded by the need to maintain a public persona as an activist while grappling with her private struggles.

Research indicates that individuals who identify as LGBTQ often experience higher rates of anxiety and depression, particularly in environments that are not supportive. According to Meyer's *Minority Stress Theory*, the chronic stress faced by LGBTQ individuals due to societal stigma can lead to various mental health issues, which in turn can affect interpersonal relationships. The internalized homophobia and societal rejection can create barriers to forming and maintaining healthy relationships.

$$\text{Mental Health} = f(\text{Minority Stress, Social Support}) \qquad (17)$$

This equation suggests that the mental health of LGBTQ individuals is a function of the stress they experience as minorities and the level of social support they receive. A lack of understanding and support from loved ones can exacerbate feelings of loneliness and despair.

## Family Dynamics

For many LGBTQ activists, family acceptance is a critical aspect of their personal lives. In the case of Wai Wai, coming out to her family was a pivotal moment. While some family members offered support, others struggled to reconcile their traditional beliefs with her identity. This dichotomy can create a rift in family dynamics, leading to conflict and emotional distance.

The impact of activism on family relationships can be profound. According to a study by *The Williams Institute*, LGBTQ individuals who are rejected by their families are more likely to experience homelessness, mental health issues, and substance abuse. Conversely, those who receive support tend to have better emotional well-being and stronger relationships.

$$\text{Family Acceptance} \propto \text{Emotional Well-being} \qquad (18)$$

This relationship illustrates that family acceptance is positively correlated with emotional well-being. For Wai Wai, the struggle for acceptance from her family was not just a personal battle; it was intertwined with her activism, as she sought to create a more inclusive society for others facing similar challenges.

## Friendships and Social Circles

Activism can also reshape friendships and social circles. As Wai Wai became more involved in LGBTQ advocacy, she found herself gravitating towards like-minded individuals who shared her passion for change. While this shift provided her with a supportive community, it also meant distancing herself from friends who did not understand or support her journey.

The phenomenon of "friendship loss" during the coming-out process is well-documented. A study published in the *Journal of Homosexuality* found that LGBTQ individuals often experience a reduction in their social networks after coming out, particularly if their friends hold conservative views. This can lead to a sense of loss and grief, as friendships that once provided comfort may become strained or dissolve entirely.

$$\text{Social Network Size} = f(\text{Supportive Friends, Activism Involvement}) \qquad (19)$$

This equation indicates that the size of an individual's social network is influenced by the presence of supportive friends and the level of involvement in activism. For Wai Wai, finding a supportive LGBTQ community was crucial in mitigating the loneliness that often accompanies activism.

## Romantic Relationships

Romantic relationships can also be significantly impacted by activism. For Wai Wai, navigating love in a conservative society posed unique challenges. The fear of public scrutiny and potential backlash could strain romantic connections, as partners might feel the weight of societal expectations. Moreover, the time and energy dedicated to activism often left little room for nurturing personal relationships.

The dynamics of romantic relationships can shift as partners grapple with the implications of activism. A study by *The American Psychological Association* highlights that LGBTQ individuals in relationships often face external pressures that can affect their bond, including discrimination and societal stigma. This external stress can lead to conflict within relationships, as partners may struggle to balance their personal lives with the demands of activism.

$$\text{Relationship Satisfaction} = f(\text{Shared Values, External Stressors}) \qquad (20)$$

This equation suggests that relationship satisfaction is influenced by shared values between partners and external stressors, such as societal discrimination. For Wai Wai, finding a partner who shared her commitment to activism was essential in fostering a supportive and understanding relationship.

## Coping Mechanisms and Resilience

Despite the challenges, many LGBTQ activists, including Wai Wai, develop coping mechanisms to navigate the complexities of their personal relationships. Building resilience through community support, therapy, and open communication can mitigate the negative impacts of activism on relationships. Engaging in dialogue with friends and family about their experiences can foster understanding and acceptance, bridging the gap between differing perspectives.

Research has shown that resilience can be cultivated through social support networks and personal coping strategies. The *Resilience Theory* posits that individuals who actively seek support and engage in positive coping mechanisms are better equipped to handle stress and maintain healthy relationships.

$$\text{Resilience} = f(\text{Social Support, Coping Strategies}) \qquad (21)$$

In conclusion, the impact of activism on personal relationships is complex and multifaceted. For Wai Wai Nu, navigating the intersection of her identity as an LGBTQ activist and her personal relationships required courage, vulnerability, and resilience. While the journey was fraught with challenges, it also opened doors to meaningful connections and a supportive community that ultimately enriched her life and advocacy efforts. The personal sacrifices made in the name of activism serve as a testament to the strength of those who dare to fight for their rights and the rights of others in the face of adversity.

# Building a LGBTQ Rights Movement in Myanmar

## Building a LGBTQ Rights Movement in Myanmar

### Building a LGBTQ Rights Movement in Myanmar

The journey toward building a robust LGBTQ rights movement in Myanmar has been fraught with challenges, yet it has also been marked by resilience and determination. The movement's foundation rests on the recognition of fundamental human rights, the importance of allyship, and the necessity of community engagement. This chapter delves into the multifaceted approach required to establish an effective LGBTQ rights movement in a country where cultural conservatism often clashes with the fight for equality.

### Engaging with Human Rights Organizations

A pivotal step in the formation of the LGBTQ rights movement in Myanmar has been the engagement with local and international human rights organizations. These organizations provide vital support through resources, advocacy, and visibility. They help amplify the voices of LGBTQ individuals and ensure that their rights are recognized as human rights.

For instance, organizations like *Human Rights Watch* and *Amnesty International* have played a crucial role in documenting abuses faced by LGBTQ individuals in Myanmar. They have also provided platforms for activists to share their stories, thereby fostering a greater understanding of the unique challenges faced by the community. The collaboration with these organizations has not only increased visibility but has also facilitated international pressure on the Myanmar government to address human rights violations.

## Acquiring Funding for LGBTQ Initiatives

Financial resources are essential for sustaining activism and creating impactful programs. Securing funding for LGBTQ initiatives in Myanmar has been a significant challenge, primarily due to societal stigma and discrimination. However, activists have successfully navigated these obstacles by forming partnerships with international NGOs and philanthropic organizations committed to human rights.

For example, grants from organizations such as *The Global Fund for Human Rights* have enabled local activists to conduct workshops, awareness campaigns, and community outreach programs. These initiatives are crucial for educating both the LGBTQ community and the broader society about human rights and the importance of acceptance.

## Collaborating with Local and International NGOs

Collaboration with NGOs has been instrumental in building a cohesive LGBTQ rights movement. Local NGOs have deep insights into the cultural context and can tailor their approaches accordingly. International NGOs, on the other hand, bring resources, expertise, and a global perspective that can enhance local efforts.

A notable example is the partnership between local activists and international organizations like *OutRight Action International*. This collaboration has led to the development of training programs that empower LGBTQ individuals with advocacy skills and knowledge about their rights. Such initiatives not only strengthen the movement but also foster a sense of community among activists.

## Partnering with Political and Religious Leaders

In a country where political and religious influences are profound, engaging with political and religious leaders is essential for advancing LGBTQ rights. Building alliances with these figures can help challenge discriminatory practices and promote inclusive policies.

For instance, some activists have successfully engaged progressive religious leaders to advocate for LGBTQ rights within their communities. By framing LGBTQ rights as a matter of compassion and human dignity, these leaders can influence public opinion and reduce stigma. Similarly, lobbying political leaders to support LGBTQ-inclusive legislation can create a more favorable environment for activism.

## Uniting LGBTQ Activists in Myanmar

Unity among LGBTQ activists is crucial for creating a strong movement. Diverse voices within the community must come together to address shared challenges and advocate for common goals. This can be achieved through regular meetings, workshops, and community events that foster collaboration and solidarity.

One successful initiative has been the establishment of an annual LGBTQ pride event, which serves as a platform for activists to unite and celebrate their identities. This event not only raises awareness but also promotes visibility, allowing activists to showcase their struggles and achievements to a broader audience.

## The Role of Education and Awareness

Education is a powerful tool in the fight for LGBTQ rights. Raising awareness about LGBTQ issues among the general population is essential for dismantling prejudices and fostering acceptance. Educational initiatives can take various forms, including workshops, public campaigns, and school programs.

For example, local activists have organized workshops in schools to educate students about sexual orientation and gender identity. These workshops aim to dispel myths and misconceptions, promoting a more inclusive understanding of LGBTQ issues. Additionally, public awareness campaigns utilizing social media have proven effective in reaching a wider audience and sparking conversations about LGBTQ rights.

## Conclusion

Building a LGBTQ rights movement in Myanmar requires a multifaceted approach that encompasses collaboration, education, and advocacy. By engaging with human rights organizations, securing funding, collaborating with NGOs, and uniting activists, the movement can create a strong foundation for change. Moreover, partnering with political and religious leaders and promoting education and awareness are crucial steps toward fostering acceptance and equality. As the movement continues to evolve, the resilience and determination of activists will be key to overcoming the challenges that lie ahead.

# Allies and Supporters

## Engaging with Human Rights Organizations

In the quest for LGBTQ rights in Myanmar, engaging with human rights organizations has proven to be a pivotal strategy for activists like Wai Wai Nu. These organizations serve as crucial allies in the fight against systemic discrimination, providing not only resources but also a platform for advocacy and visibility.

The collaboration with human rights organizations can be understood through several key theoretical frameworks. One such framework is the **Social Movement Theory**, which posits that collective action is essential for social change. According to this theory, movements gain momentum when they can effectively mobilize resources, build networks, and create public awareness. Human rights organizations play a vital role in this process by offering logistical support, training, and funding, which are essential for grassroots activism.

A significant problem faced by LGBTQ activists in Myanmar is the pervasive stigma and discrimination that limits their ability to organize and advocate openly. This is exacerbated by the legal framework that criminalizes same-sex relationships, creating an environment of fear and repression. Engaging with established human rights organizations can help mitigate these challenges. For instance, organizations such as *Human Rights Watch* and *Amnesty International* have a global platform that can amplify local voices, drawing international attention to the struggles faced by LGBTQ individuals in Myanmar.

An example of effective engagement is the partnership between local LGBTQ groups and international NGOs. In 2015, a coalition of activists collaborated with *OutRight Action International* to document human rights abuses against LGBTQ individuals in Myanmar. This collaboration not only provided a comprehensive report that was presented to the United Nations but also empowered local activists by equipping them with the necessary skills to document abuses and advocate for their rights.

Furthermore, human rights organizations often have established networks that can facilitate connections between local activists and global allies. This network building is crucial for sustaining momentum in advocacy efforts. For example, during the annual *International Human Rights Day* celebrations, local LGBTQ activists in Myanmar have been able to participate in global campaigns organized by human rights organizations, thereby increasing visibility and solidarity.

However, the engagement with human rights organizations is not without its challenges. One significant issue is the potential for **tokenism**, where local voices are overshadowed by international narratives. To combat this, it is essential that human rights organizations prioritize the leadership and perspectives of local activists. This can be achieved by fostering genuine partnerships that allow for shared decision-making and strategy development.

Moreover, the intersectionality of LGBTQ rights with other human rights issues must be recognized. Activists in Myanmar often face overlapping challenges related to ethnicity, gender, and socio-economic status. Human rights organizations must adopt an intersectional approach, recognizing that the fight for LGBTQ rights cannot be separated from broader struggles for human rights and social justice. This approach not only enhances the effectiveness of advocacy efforts but also builds a more inclusive movement.

In conclusion, engaging with human rights organizations is a multifaceted strategy that can significantly bolster the fight for LGBTQ rights in Myanmar. By leveraging the resources, networks, and platforms provided by these organizations, local activists can amplify their voices, challenge discriminatory laws, and foster a culture of acceptance and equality. As Wai Wai Nu and her fellow activists continue to navigate the complexities of advocacy in a conservative society, the support of human rights organizations remains an invaluable asset in their pursuit of justice and recognition.

## Acquiring Funding for LGBTQ Initiatives

Acquiring funding for LGBTQ initiatives in Myanmar presents a unique set of challenges and opportunities. The socio-political landscape, characterized by traditional values and legal barriers against LGBTQ rights, complicates the quest for financial support. However, understanding the dynamics of funding sources, the importance of strategic partnerships, and the effective use of resources can significantly enhance the viability of LGBTQ initiatives.

### Understanding Funding Sources

The first step in acquiring funding is to identify potential sources. Funding for LGBTQ initiatives can be categorized into several types:

+ **International Grants:** Many international organizations, such as the Global Fund for Human Rights and the Open Society Foundations, offer grants specifically aimed at supporting LGBTQ rights. These grants often require detailed proposals that outline the objectives, expected outcomes, and methodologies of the initiative.

+ **Local NGOs and Philanthropy:** Local non-governmental organizations (NGOs) may provide funding or resources for LGBTQ initiatives. Building relationships with these organizations can lead to collaborative funding opportunities.

+ **Crowdfunding:** Platforms like GoFundMe or Kickstarter have emerged as viable options for grassroots fundraising. Successful campaigns often rely on compelling narratives and community engagement to attract small donations from a broad audience.

+ **Corporate Sponsorship:** Some businesses are increasingly recognizing the importance of corporate social responsibility (CSR) and may be willing to sponsor LGBTQ events or initiatives. Establishing partnerships with LGBTQ-friendly companies can lead to financial support and increased visibility.

## The Importance of Strategic Partnerships

Strategic partnerships are crucial for acquiring funding. Collaborating with established organizations can enhance credibility and attract larger grants. For example, when Wai Wai Nu partnered with international NGOs, they not only gained access to funding but also benefited from their expertise in advocacy and program development. This collaboration allowed for a more robust framework in which initiatives could be implemented effectively.

## Challenges in Acquiring Funding

Despite the availability of various funding sources, LGBTQ initiatives in Myanmar face significant challenges:

+ **Stigma and Discrimination:** The prevailing stigma surrounding LGBTQ issues can deter potential funders. Many organizations may hesitate to support initiatives in regions where LGBTQ rights are not recognized, fearing backlash or reputational damage.

+ **Legal Barriers:** The criminalization of homosexuality in Myanmar creates a risky environment for funders. Legal repercussions for supporting LGBTQ initiatives can lead to reluctance from international organizations, further complicating funding efforts.

+ **Limited Awareness:** There is often a lack of awareness about LGBTQ issues among potential funders. This gap necessitates education and advocacy to inform funders about the importance of supporting LGBTQ rights and initiatives.

## Successful Examples of Funding Initiatives

Several successful examples illustrate effective strategies for acquiring funding:

+ **The Myanmar LGBTQ Network:** This coalition successfully secured funding through a combination of international grants and local partnerships. By presenting a united front, they were able to demonstrate the collective impact of their initiatives, attracting attention and resources from various funders.

+ **Community Engagement Campaigns:** Initiatives that involve community members in fundraising efforts have proven effective. For instance, organizing events such as pride parades or awareness campaigns not only raise funds but also foster community solidarity and visibility.

+ **Digital Fundraising Strategies:** Utilizing social media platforms to share personal stories and highlight the importance of LGBTQ initiatives has led to successful crowdfunding campaigns. Engaging narratives can resonate with a broader audience and encourage donations.

## Conclusion

Acquiring funding for LGBTQ initiatives in Myanmar is a multifaceted endeavor that requires a strategic approach, awareness of challenges, and the ability to forge meaningful partnerships. By leveraging a diverse array of funding sources and engaging the community, LGBTQ activists can create sustainable initiatives that foster change and promote equality. As the movement for LGBTQ rights continues to grow, the need for financial support remains critical in the fight for acceptance and legal recognition in Myanmar.

## Collaborating with Local and International NGOs

The collaboration between LGBTQ activists and both local and international non-governmental organizations (NGOs) plays a pivotal role in advancing the rights and well-being of LGBTQ individuals in Myanmar. This partnership not only amplifies the voices of marginalized communities but also facilitates the exchange of resources, knowledge, and strategies that are crucial for effective advocacy.

## The Importance of Collaboration

In a country where LGBTQ rights are severely restricted, the need for a robust support system is paramount.    Local NGOs often possess an intimate understanding of the cultural and socio-political landscape, which enables them to tailor their approaches to the unique challenges faced by LGBTQ individuals. Conversely, international NGOs bring a wealth of experience from other contexts, along with access to broader networks and funding opportunities. This synergy can enhance the effectiveness of advocacy efforts.

## Challenges in Collaboration

Despite the clear benefits, collaboration is not without its challenges.    One significant issue is the potential for cultural misalignment.  International NGOs may inadvertently impose Western ideologies that do not resonate with local realities, leading to resistance from the communities they aim to help.  Moreover, local NGOs may struggle with limited resources and capacity, making it difficult to engage effectively with larger organizations.

## Strategies for Effective Collaboration

To maximize the impact of these partnerships, several strategies can be employed:

- **Cultural Sensitivity Training:** Both local and international NGOs should prioritize understanding each other's cultural contexts. This can be achieved through workshops and training sessions that focus on the nuances of LGBTQ issues in Myanmar, fostering mutual respect and collaboration.

- **Joint Initiatives:** Developing joint initiatives can help bridge the gap between local and international organizations. For example, a local NGO might collaborate with an international partner to organize an LGBTQ rights awareness campaign, combining local insights with global best practices.

- **Resource Sharing:** Local NGOs can benefit from the funding and technical expertise of international organizations. Conversely, international NGOs can gain credibility and community trust by partnering with established local entities. This reciprocal relationship can enhance the sustainability of initiatives.

✦ **Capacity Building:** International NGOs should focus on capacity building within local organizations, providing training and resources that empower them to lead initiatives independently. This fosters long-term sustainability and resilience within the local LGBTQ movement.

## Examples of Successful Collaborations

Several successful collaborations illustrate the potential of these partnerships. For instance, the organization *Rainbow Myanmar* has effectively partnered with international NGOs like *OutRight Action International* to conduct training workshops for LGBTQ activists. These workshops have equipped activists with essential skills in advocacy, media engagement, and legal rights, significantly enhancing their effectiveness in the local context.

Another notable example is the collaboration between local health NGOs and international organizations to address the health needs of LGBTQ individuals in Myanmar. By working together, they have successfully implemented programs that provide HIV prevention and treatment services tailored to the LGBTQ community, demonstrating the power of collaborative efforts in addressing specific community needs.

## Conclusion

In conclusion, the collaboration between local and international NGOs is crucial for the advancement of LGBTQ rights in Myanmar. By leveraging each other's strengths, these organizations can create a more inclusive and supportive environment for LGBTQ individuals. However, it is essential to navigate the challenges of cultural differences and resource limitations with sensitivity and a commitment to mutual empowerment. As these partnerships continue to evolve, they hold the potential to foster a more equitable society where LGBTQ individuals can thrive without fear of discrimination or violence.

## Partnering with Political and Religious Leaders

In the journey toward establishing a robust LGBTQ rights movement in Myanmar, the importance of strategic partnerships cannot be overstated. Engaging with political and religious leaders has emerged as a crucial avenue for fostering understanding, dismantling prejudices, and advocating for legal reforms. The intersection of politics, religion, and LGBTQ rights in Myanmar presents both opportunities and challenges that must be navigated with care and insight.

## The Role of Political Leaders

Political leaders hold significant power in shaping public policy and societal norms. In Myanmar, where political landscapes can shift rapidly, cultivating relationships with key political figures is essential for advancing LGBTQ rights.

**Building Alliances**   Establishing alliances with progressive political leaders can create a supportive environment for LGBTQ initiatives. For instance, during the 2015 elections, various LGBTQ activists engaged with candidates who expressed a commitment to human rights. By leveraging these relationships, activists were able to advocate for inclusive policies that addressed discrimination and promoted equality.

**Challenges Faced**   However, the challenge lies in the fact that many political leaders may harbor traditional beliefs that conflict with LGBTQ rights.   For example, in a country where conservative values are deeply entrenched, openly advocating for LGBTQ rights can be politically risky.   Activists must approach these partnerships with a strategy that emphasizes mutual benefits, such as highlighting the economic advantages of inclusivity or the potential for increased tourism through a more accepting society.

## Engaging Religious Leaders

Religion plays a pivotal role in shaping societal attitudes in Myanmar. Engaging religious leaders can be a double-edged sword, as their influence can either hinder or help the progress of LGBTQ rights.

**Finding Common Ground**   Some religious leaders have begun to advocate for compassion and acceptance, recognizing the need for love and understanding within their communities. For instance, certain Buddhist leaders have spoken out against discrimination, framing their arguments within the context of compassion and human dignity. By partnering with these progressive voices, LGBTQ activists can work to change the narrative surrounding LGBTQ individuals in religious communities.

**Addressing Opposition**    Conversely, many religious leaders may oppose LGBTQ rights, citing traditional beliefs and doctrines. This opposition can manifest in public statements and actions that reinforce discrimination. Activists must navigate these complexities by engaging in dialogue that seeks to educate and inform, while also respecting the deeply held beliefs of religious communities.

## Examples of Successful Partnerships

Successful partnerships between LGBTQ activists and political/religious leaders have been documented in various contexts. For example, in 2019, a coalition of LGBTQ activists partnered with a progressive political party to advocate for the repeal of discriminatory laws. This collaboration not only raised awareness but also garnered significant media attention, putting pressure on lawmakers to consider reform.

Similarly, interfaith dialogues have emerged as a powerful tool for bridging gaps between LGBTQ communities and religious groups. By creating safe spaces for discussion, activists have been able to foster understanding and build alliances that transcend traditional boundaries.

## Theoretical Framework

The theoretical underpinnings of these partnerships can be analyzed through the lens of social movement theory, particularly the concepts of resource mobilization and political opportunity structures. Resource mobilization theory posits that successful movements require access to resources, including political connections. By partnering with influential leaders, LGBTQ activists can enhance their resource base, facilitating more effective advocacy.

Political opportunity structures, on the other hand, emphasize the importance of the political environment in which movements operate. Engaging with political and religious leaders can alter these structures, creating openings for dialogue and reform that may not have existed previously.

## Conclusion

In conclusion, partnering with political and religious leaders is a multifaceted strategy that offers both opportunities and challenges for LGBTQ activists in Myanmar. By building alliances with progressive figures and engaging in constructive dialogue with traditional leaders, activists can foster a more inclusive society. As these partnerships evolve, they hold the potential to reshape public perceptions, influence policy, and ultimately pave the way for a more equitable future for LGBTQ individuals in Myanmar. The journey is fraught with obstacles, but the commitment to collaboration and understanding can lead to meaningful change.

## Uniting LGBTQ Activists in Myanmar

The journey toward LGBTQ rights in Myanmar has been fraught with challenges, yet it has also fostered a remarkable spirit of unity among activists. Uniting LGBTQ activists is not merely a strategic move; it is a necessity in a country where societal norms and legal frameworks often marginalize and criminalize diverse sexual orientations and gender identities. This section explores the significance of solidarity among LGBTQ activists in Myanmar, the theoretical frameworks that underpin collective action, and the practical steps taken to foster unity.

### Theoretical Frameworks of Collective Action

Collective action theory provides a foundational understanding of how individuals come together to achieve common goals. According to Mancur Olson's theory of collective action, individuals are more likely to participate in movements when they perceive that their interests align with those of the group. In the context of LGBTQ activism in Myanmar, the shared experiences of discrimination and marginalization create a compelling impetus for collective action.

Furthermore, social identity theory posits that individuals derive a sense of self from their membership in social groups. For LGBTQ individuals in Myanmar, identifying as part of a broader community not only fosters resilience but also enhances the visibility of their struggles. This sense of belonging is crucial in a society where many face ostracism and hostility.

### Challenges to Unity

Despite the compelling reasons for unity, LGBTQ activists in Myanmar encounter several challenges that threaten their collective efforts. One significant barrier is the diversity within the LGBTQ community itself. Differences in ethnicity, socioeconomic status, and gender identity can create divisions that hinder collaboration. For example, the experiences of a gay man from Yangon may differ significantly from those of a transgender woman from a rural area, leading to varying priorities and approaches to activism.

Moreover, the pervasive fear of persecution can lead to a reluctance to engage openly with others. Activists often navigate a landscape of threats and harassment, making it difficult to build trust and foster collaboration. The internalized stigma associated with being LGBTQ in a conservative society can further complicate efforts to unite.

## Practical Steps for Uniting Activists

To overcome these challenges, several strategies have been implemented to unite LGBTQ activists in Myanmar:

+ **Creating Safe Spaces:** Establishing safe spaces for dialogue and collaboration is essential. Organizations have begun hosting workshops and retreats where activists can share their experiences and build solidarity. These gatherings not only facilitate communication but also help to cultivate a sense of community.

+ **Developing Intersectional Approaches:** Recognizing the diversity within the LGBTQ community is crucial for fostering unity. Activists are increasingly adopting intersectional approaches that address the unique challenges faced by various subgroups. For instance, initiatives that specifically focus on the rights of transgender individuals or ethnic minorities within the LGBTQ community can bridge gaps and promote inclusivity.

+ **Utilizing Technology:** In an age where digital communication is prevalent, social media platforms have become vital tools for uniting activists. Online forums, social media groups, and virtual meetings allow activists from different regions to connect, share resources, and strategize collectively, regardless of geographical barriers.

+ **Collaborative Campaigns:** Joint campaigns that highlight shared goals can serve as powerful unifying forces. By organizing events such as pride parades, awareness campaigns, or fundraising efforts, activists can demonstrate solidarity and amplify their voices. Such collaborative efforts not only raise awareness but also foster a sense of collective identity.

+ **Building Alliances with Allies:** Engaging allies from outside the LGBTQ community can bolster unity. Collaborating with human rights organizations, feminist groups, and other social justice movements can create a broader coalition advocating for change. This intersectional solidarity can enhance visibility and amplify the demands for LGBTQ rights.

## Examples of Successful Unity

Several instances illustrate the power of unity among LGBTQ activists in Myanmar. One notable example is the formation of the *Pride Network*, a coalition of LGBTQ organizations that emerged in response to the need for a unified front against discrimination. This network has successfully organized events that not only celebrate LGBTQ identities but also advocate for legal reforms.

Additionally, during the COVID-19 pandemic, various LGBTQ organizations collaborated to provide essential services to vulnerable community members. By pooling resources and expertise, they were able to offer support that addressed both health and economic challenges faced by LGBTQ individuals during this crisis.

## Conclusion

Uniting LGBTQ activists in Myanmar is a multifaceted endeavor that requires navigating challenges while fostering solidarity. By embracing collective action theories, addressing internal divisions, and implementing practical strategies, activists can build a more cohesive movement. The journey toward LGBTQ rights in Myanmar is ongoing, but through unity, resilience, and collaboration, there is hope for a brighter future where all individuals can live authentically and without fear.

# Education and Awareness

## LGBTQ-Inclusive Education

LGBTQ-inclusive education is a crucial component in the fight for equality and acceptance within society, particularly in conservative environments like Myanmar. This section explores the theory behind LGBTQ-inclusive education, the existing problems that hinder its implementation, and examples of successful initiatives that have made a significant impact.

## Theoretical Framework

The foundation of LGBTQ-inclusive education rests on the principles of social justice and equality. According to [?], education should not only impart knowledge but also challenge systemic inequalities and promote critical thinking. Incorporating LGBTQ perspectives into educational curricula aligns with the broader goals of multicultural education, which seeks to recognize and validate diverse identities and experiences [?].

The *Social Learning Theory* posits that individuals learn behaviors, norms, and values through observation and imitation [?]. By exposing students to LGBTQ-inclusive narratives, schools can foster empathy and understanding, reducing prejudice and discrimination. Furthermore, the *Queer Theory* emphasizes the fluidity of identity and challenges the binary understanding of gender and sexuality, advocating for a more inclusive approach to education [?].

## Challenges in Implementation

Despite the clear benefits of LGBTQ-inclusive education, several challenges hinder its implementation in Myanmar.

+ **Cultural Resistance:** The deeply ingrained traditional values and norms often lead to resistance from parents, educators, and policymakers. Many view LGBTQ topics as taboo or contrary to cultural and religious beliefs, which can result in pushback against inclusive curricula.

+ **Lack of Training:** Educators often lack the necessary training to address LGBTQ issues sensitively and effectively. Without proper professional development, teachers may feel ill-equipped to handle discussions around gender and sexuality, leading to avoidance or misinformation.

+ **Limited Resources:** Educational institutions frequently lack access to LGBTQ-inclusive materials and resources. The absence of textbooks, teaching aids, and training programs that address LGBTQ issues further perpetuates ignorance and stigma.

+ **Legal Barriers:** The criminalization of homosexuality in Myanmar creates a hostile environment for LGBTQ individuals and advocates. This legal framework not only fosters discrimination but also discourages educational institutions from adopting inclusive practices due to fear of repercussions.

## Examples of Successful Initiatives

Despite these challenges, there have been notable efforts to promote LGBTQ-inclusive education in Myanmar:

+ **Workshops and Training Programs:** Organizations such as *Equality Myanmar* have initiated workshops aimed at training educators on LGBTQ issues. These programs provide educators with the tools and knowledge necessary to create a more inclusive classroom environment, fostering understanding and acceptance among students.

+ **Curriculum Development:** Collaborations between local NGOs and educational institutions have led to the development of LGBTQ-inclusive curricula. For example, integrating LGBTQ history and literature into existing subjects not only educates students about diverse identities but also encourages critical discussions about social justice and human rights.

+ **Peer Education Programs:** Empowering LGBTQ youth to act as peer educators within schools has proven effective in promoting acceptance. Programs that train LGBTQ youth to share their experiences and educate their peers help reduce stigma and foster a more inclusive school culture.

+ **International Partnerships:** Collaborating with international organizations can provide vital resources and support for LGBTQ-inclusive education initiatives. For instance, partnerships with global LGBTQ advocacy groups can facilitate the sharing of best practices and educational materials tailored to the local context.

## Conclusion

In conclusion, LGBTQ-inclusive education is essential for fostering a culture of acceptance and understanding in Myanmar. While significant challenges remain, the theoretical framework supporting inclusive education, combined with successful initiatives, provides a roadmap for progress. By prioritizing LGBTQ-inclusive education, Myanmar can take critical steps toward dismantling prejudice and discrimination, ultimately paving the way for a more equitable society.

## Conducting Workshops and Training Programs

In the pursuit of advancing LGBTQ rights in Myanmar, conducting workshops and training programs has emerged as a pivotal strategy for fostering awareness and understanding within communities. These initiatives serve not only to educate participants about LGBTQ issues but also to empower them to become advocates for change. This section explores the theoretical underpinnings, challenges, and successful examples of such programs.

## Theoretical Framework

The foundation for conducting effective workshops lies in several educational theories, including andragogy, experiential learning, and transformative learning theory.

+ **Andragogy** emphasizes the importance of self-directed learning in adults. It posits that adults learn best when they can relate the material to their own experiences. Therefore, workshops should be designed to engage participants actively, encouraging them to share their stories and perspectives.

+ **Experiential Learning Theory** suggests that knowledge is created through the transformation of experience. This theory supports the use of role-playing, simulations, and interactive exercises in workshops to help participants understand complex issues related to LGBTQ rights.

+ **Transformative Learning Theory** focuses on the process of change in beliefs and perspectives. Workshops can facilitate transformative learning by challenging preconceived notions about gender and sexuality, allowing participants to reflect critically on their own biases and assumptions.

## Identifying Problems and Challenges

While the potential for workshops to create positive change is significant, several challenges can impede their effectiveness:

+ **Cultural Resistance:** In a traditional society like Myanmar, entrenched cultural norms often lead to resistance against LGBTQ topics. Participants may arrive with preconceived notions that hinder open dialogue.

+ **Safety Concerns:** Given the legal and social risks associated with LGBTQ identities in Myanmar, participants may fear repercussions for attending workshops. Ensuring a safe and confidential environment is crucial for fostering honest discussions.

+ **Resource Limitations:** Limited funding and resources can restrict the scope of workshops. This can affect the quality of materials, facilitators, and venues, ultimately impacting participant engagement and learning outcomes.

## Successful Examples

Despite these challenges, numerous successful workshops have been implemented throughout Myanmar, demonstrating the effectiveness of this approach:

- **Youth Empowerment Workshops:** In collaboration with local NGOs, workshops targeting youth have been conducted in urban centers like Yangon. These workshops focus on self-acceptance, the importance of allyship, and understanding LGBTQ rights. Activities include group discussions, role-playing scenarios, and creative expression through art, allowing participants to explore their identities safely.

- **Community Leader Training:** Workshops aimed at training community leaders have proven effective in amplifying LGBTQ voices within broader social movements. By equipping leaders with knowledge about LGBTQ rights and advocacy strategies, these programs foster allyship and support within various community sectors, including religious and political organizations.

- **Health and Wellness Workshops:** Recognizing the unique health needs of LGBTQ individuals, workshops have been developed to educate healthcare providers on LGBTQ-specific issues. These sessions address topics such as mental health, sexual health, and the importance of inclusive healthcare practices, ultimately improving access to services for marginalized communities.

## Evaluation and Impact Assessment

To ensure the effectiveness of workshops, it is essential to implement evaluation mechanisms. This can include pre- and post-workshop surveys to assess changes in knowledge, attitudes, and behaviors. For example, a workshop might measure participants' understanding of LGBTQ rights before and after the session, using a simple scoring system:

$$\text{Knowledge Gain} = \frac{\text{Post-Test Score} - \text{Pre-Test Score}}{\text{Pre-Test Score}} \times 100\% \qquad (22)$$

Such evaluations provide valuable feedback for refining future workshops and demonstrating their impact to potential funders and partners.

## Conclusion

Conducting workshops and training programs is a vital component of building an inclusive LGBTQ rights movement in Myanmar. By leveraging educational theories, addressing challenges, and learning from successful examples, these initiatives can effectively empower individuals and communities to advocate for LGBTQ rights. As more people become educated and engaged, the movement towards equality and acceptance continues to gain momentum, transforming societal attitudes and paving the way for lasting change.

# Developing LGBTQ Resources and Materials

The development of LGBTQ resources and materials is crucial in fostering understanding, acceptance, and advocacy within society. In Myanmar, where cultural and societal norms often marginalize LGBTQ individuals, creating accessible and relevant resources is not only a necessity but a powerful tool for activism.

## The Importance of Resources

Resources such as pamphlets, brochures, educational videos, and online content serve multiple purposes. They inform the public about LGBTQ issues, provide support for individuals questioning their sexual orientation or gender identity, and offer guidance on legal rights and health services. The creation of these materials can help combat misinformation and stereotypes, which are prevalent in conservative societies.

## Identifying Key Topics

When developing resources, it is essential to identify key topics that resonate with the local LGBTQ community. These may include:

+ **Understanding Sexual Orientation and Gender Identity:** Educational materials should clarify the differences between sexual orientation and gender identity, emphasizing that both are valid aspects of human diversity.

+ **Legal Rights and Protections:** Informational resources must outline the current legal landscape regarding LGBTQ rights in Myanmar, including any protections available and the legal ramifications of discrimination.

- **Mental Health and Well-being:** Resources should address the mental health challenges faced by LGBTQ individuals, offering strategies for coping with stigma and discrimination.

- **Health Resources:** Providing information on LGBTQ-friendly healthcare services, sexual health education, and access to mental health support is vital for the community's well-being.

## Collaborative Development Process

The process of developing these resources should be collaborative, involving input from LGBTQ individuals, activists, mental health professionals, and educators. This approach ensures that the materials are relevant, culturally sensitive, and reflective of the community's needs. For instance, workshops can be organized where community members share their experiences and insights, which can then be translated into resource materials.

## Utilizing Technology and Media

In the digital age, utilizing technology to disseminate resources is paramount. Online platforms can host educational videos, webinars, and forums where individuals can seek guidance and support anonymously. For example, a dedicated website or social media page can serve as a hub for sharing information about LGBTQ rights, upcoming events, and available resources.

Moreover, the use of infographics and visual storytelling can make complex information more digestible. Visual materials can be particularly effective in engaging younger audiences who are more likely to consume content online.

## Challenges in Resource Development

Despite the need for comprehensive resources, several challenges may arise during the development process:

- **Censorship and Restrictions:** In many cases, governmental restrictions on LGBTQ content may hinder the creation and distribution of materials. Activists must navigate these challenges carefully to ensure that resources reach their intended audience without facing legal repercussions.

- **Cultural Sensitivity:** Resources must be developed with a deep understanding of local cultural contexts to avoid backlash. This requires continuous dialogue with community members to ensure that materials are respectful and appropriate.

+ **Funding and Support:** Securing funding for the development of resources can be a significant barrier. Many LGBTQ initiatives rely on grants and donations, which may be limited. Building partnerships with local NGOs and international organizations can help alleviate this issue.

## Examples of Successful Resource Initiatives

Several successful initiatives can serve as models for developing LGBTQ resources in Myanmar:

+ **The Rainbow Resource Center:** This initiative created a comprehensive guide for LGBTQ individuals that covers legal rights, mental health resources, and community support. The guide is available in both print and digital formats, ensuring accessibility.

+ **LGBTQ Health Awareness Campaigns:** Collaborations with health organizations have led to the development of materials that address sexual health specifically for LGBTQ individuals. These materials include pamphlets distributed in clinics and community centers.

+ **Educational Workshops in Schools:** Programs that introduce LGBTQ topics into school curricula have proven effective in raising awareness among young people. These workshops often include resource materials that students can take home.

## Conclusion

Developing LGBTQ resources and materials is a critical component of advocacy in Myanmar. By focusing on relevant topics, engaging the community in the development process, and leveraging technology, activists can create impactful materials that educate, empower, and inspire change. Despite the challenges, the potential for positive impact is immense, paving the way for a more inclusive and accepting society.

## Advocating for LGBTQ-Inclusive Policies in Schools

In the fight for LGBTQ rights, education plays a pivotal role in shaping attitudes and fostering acceptance among future generations. Advocating for

LGBTQ-inclusive policies in schools not only addresses the immediate needs of LGBTQ students but also helps to cultivate a culture of understanding and respect that can permeate society as a whole. This section delves into the theoretical foundations, challenges, and practical examples of advocating for such policies within educational institutions.

## Theoretical Foundations

The advocacy for LGBTQ-inclusive policies in schools is grounded in several key theories, including Social Justice Theory and Queer Theory. Social Justice Theory emphasizes the importance of equity and fairness in education, arguing that all students, regardless of their sexual orientation or gender identity, deserve a safe and supportive learning environment. According to this theory, inclusive policies are essential for dismantling systemic inequalities that marginalize LGBTQ students.

Queer Theory, on the other hand, challenges the binary understanding of gender and sexuality, advocating for a more fluid interpretation of identity. This theoretical perspective supports the need for schools to recognize and validate diverse identities, thereby affirming the experiences of LGBTQ individuals. By integrating these theories into educational policy, advocates can promote a more inclusive and affirming school climate.

## Challenges to LGBTQ-Inclusive Policies

Despite the clear benefits of LGBTQ-inclusive policies, several challenges hinder their implementation in schools. These challenges can be categorized into societal, institutional, and individual barriers:

- **Societal Barriers:** Deep-rooted cultural norms and prejudices often manifest in resistance to LGBTQ-inclusive policies. In many communities, discussing issues of gender and sexuality remains taboo, leading to pushback from parents and local organizations. This resistance can create a hostile environment for both students and educators advocating for change.

- **Institutional Barriers:** School administrations may lack the resources or training necessary to implement inclusive policies effectively. Additionally, existing curricula often overlook LGBTQ topics, leaving educators without guidance on how to address these issues in the classroom. This lack of institutional support can stifle efforts to create inclusive environments.

+ **Individual Barriers:** Educators may feel unprepared or fearful to engage with LGBTQ issues due to their own biases or lack of knowledge. This fear can lead to avoidance of LGBTQ topics, further perpetuating an environment of silence and exclusion.

## Examples of Advocacy in Action

Despite these challenges, numerous successful initiatives demonstrate the potential for advocating LGBTQ-inclusive policies in schools. These examples highlight effective strategies and the positive impact of inclusive practices:

+ **Safe Schools Coalition:** This initiative, which began in Australia, works to create safe and supportive environments for LGBTQ students. By providing resources, training, and advocacy support, the Coalition has successfully influenced policy changes in numerous schools, resulting in the implementation of anti-bullying programs and the inclusion of LGBTQ topics in the curriculum.

+ **GSA (Gay-Straight Alliance) Clubs:** Many schools have established GSA clubs, which serve as safe spaces for LGBTQ students and their allies. These clubs not only provide support but also engage in advocacy efforts to promote inclusive policies within their schools. For example, GSAs have successfully lobbied for the inclusion of LGBTQ history in social studies curricula, fostering greater awareness and understanding among the student body.

+ **LGBTQ-Inclusive Curriculum Development:** Some school districts have taken proactive steps to develop LGBTQ-inclusive curricula. For instance, the Massachusetts Department of Elementary and Secondary Education has implemented guidelines that encourage the integration of LGBTQ content across various subjects, from literature to health education. This approach not only validates LGBTQ identities but also educates all students about diversity and inclusion.

+ **Policy Frameworks:** Organizations like the Human Rights Campaign have developed comprehensive policy frameworks that schools can adopt to ensure LGBTQ inclusivity. These frameworks outline best practices for creating safe environments, addressing bullying, and implementing inclusive curricula. Schools that adopt these frameworks often report a decrease in incidents of bullying and an increase in student well-being.

## Conclusion

Advocating for LGBTQ-inclusive policies in schools is a critical component of fostering an equitable and just educational environment. By addressing the theoretical foundations, recognizing the challenges, and learning from successful examples, advocates can work to create schools that not only accept but celebrate diversity. As we strive for a more inclusive future, it is imperative that educators, administrators, and policymakers collaborate to ensure that every student, regardless of their sexual orientation or gender identity, feels safe, valued, and empowered to thrive.

The journey toward LGBTQ-inclusive education is ongoing, but with persistent advocacy and community support, meaningful change is not only possible but essential. By prioritizing the needs of LGBTQ students, we can cultivate a generation that embraces diversity and champions equality for all.

## Promoting Acceptance and Understanding

Promoting acceptance and understanding of LGBTQ individuals in Myanmar is a crucial aspect of building an inclusive society. This endeavor not only challenges existing prejudices but also fosters a culture of empathy and respect. The following key strategies are essential in this process:

### Education as a Tool for Change

Education plays a pivotal role in shaping societal attitudes. Research indicates that comprehensive LGBTQ-inclusive education can significantly reduce homophobic attitudes among students (Herek, 2009). By integrating LGBTQ topics into the school curriculum, educators can challenge stereotypes and foster a more accepting environment. For instance, workshops that address LGBTQ history, rights, and contributions can help demystify LGBTQ identities and promote understanding.

### Community Engagement and Dialogue

Creating opportunities for open dialogue between LGBTQ individuals and the broader community is vital. Community forums and discussions can serve as platforms for sharing personal stories, which humanize LGBTQ experiences and dispel myths. For example, organizing events where LGBTQ activists share their journeys can create a space for empathy and connection. This aligns with the contact hypothesis, which posits that interpersonal contact can reduce prejudice (Allport, 1954).

## Media Representation

Media representation is another powerful tool in promoting acceptance. Positive portrayals of LGBTQ individuals in local media can challenge negative stereotypes and foster a sense of belonging. Campaigns that highlight LGBTQ achievements and contributions to society can shift public perception. For instance, featuring LGBTQ role models in television programs or social media campaigns can inspire acceptance and pride within the community.

## Partnerships with Religious Institutions

Engaging with religious leaders and institutions can also be transformative. In many cultures, religion plays a significant role in shaping attitudes towards LGBTQ individuals. By fostering dialogue between LGBTQ advocates and religious leaders, it is possible to promote interpretations of faith that embrace inclusivity. Initiatives that focus on common values such as love, compassion, and acceptance can bridge gaps and reduce discrimination.

## Utilizing Social Media Platforms

In the digital age, social media serves as a powerful tool for advocacy and education. Campaigns that utilize platforms like Facebook, Instagram, and Twitter can reach a wide audience, promoting messages of acceptance and understanding. For instance, hashtags such as #LoveIsLove and #Pride can galvanize support and create a sense of community. Engaging content, such as videos and infographics, can effectively communicate the importance of LGBTQ rights and foster empathy.

## The Role of Allies

Allies play a crucial role in promoting acceptance. By using their privilege to advocate for LGBTQ rights, allies can amplify marginalized voices and challenge discriminatory practices. Training programs for allies can equip them with the tools to effectively support LGBTQ individuals, fostering a culture of solidarity. For example, workshops that educate allies on LGBTQ issues and how to be supportive can create a more inclusive environment.

## Challenges to Acceptance

Despite these efforts, promoting acceptance and understanding is fraught with challenges. Deep-rooted cultural norms and prejudices can hinder progress. Many individuals may resist change due to fear or misinformation. Additionally, the lack of LGBTQ representation in decision-making processes can perpetuate discrimination.    Addressing these challenges requires sustained efforts and collaboration among various stakeholders.

## Conclusion

Promoting acceptance and understanding of LGBTQ individuals in Myanmar is an ongoing journey that necessitates collective action.    By leveraging education, community engagement, media representation, and allyship, it is possible to create a more inclusive society.    As Wai Wai Nu and other activists continue to advocate for LGBTQ rights, the vision of a society rooted in acceptance and understanding becomes increasingly attainable.

# Bibliography

[1]  Herek, G. M. (2009). *Sexual Stigma and Sexual Prejudice in the United States: A Conceptual Framework*. Archives of Sexual Behavior, 38(5), 976-988.

[2]  Allport, G. W. (1954). *The Nature of Prejudice*. Addison-Wesley.

## Fighting Legal Discrimination

### The Criminalization of Homosexuality in Myanmar

The issue of homosexuality in Myanmar is deeply intertwined with the country's legal framework, cultural norms, and historical context. The criminalization of homosexual acts is primarily rooted in the colonial-era laws that have persisted into modern times. Specifically, Section 377 of the Penal Code, inherited from British colonial rule, criminalizes "carnal intercourse against the order of nature," which has been interpreted to include same-sex relations. This legal framework not only stigmatizes LGBTQ individuals but also perpetuates a culture of discrimination and violence against them.

### Historical Context

To understand the current state of LGBTQ rights in Myanmar, it is essential to consider the historical context. The British colonial administration implemented laws that targeted sexual minorities, and these laws remained largely unchanged after Myanmar gained independence in 1948. The legal system in Myanmar has continued to reflect these colonial legacies, with little progress made toward decriminalization. The persistence of these laws has contributed to a societal perception that views homosexuality as deviant, leading to widespread discrimination and marginalization.

## Legal Framework and Enforcement

The enforcement of Section 377 is often arbitrary and can vary significantly across different regions of Myanmar. While the law is rarely invoked in urban areas, it remains a tool for oppression in more conservative and rural communities. Police harassment, extortion, and violence against LGBTQ individuals are common, with many cases going unreported due to fear of further victimization. The lack of legal protections for LGBTQ individuals creates a climate of fear, stifling activism and discouraging individuals from seeking justice.

## Impact on LGBTQ Individuals

The criminalization of homosexuality has severe implications for the mental and physical well-being of LGBTQ individuals in Myanmar. Many face societal ostracism, familial rejection, and violence, which can lead to mental health issues such as depression and anxiety. The fear of being outed or prosecuted often forces individuals to live in secrecy, leading to a sense of isolation and hopelessness. This environment undermines the potential for community building and solidarity among LGBTQ individuals, further perpetuating their marginalization.

## International Human Rights Perspective

From an international human rights perspective, the criminalization of homosexuality is a violation of fundamental human rights. Various human rights organizations, including Amnesty International and Human Rights Watch, have condemned the laws in Myanmar, calling for their repeal. The United Nations has also emphasized that criminalizing same-sex relationships is inconsistent with international human rights standards, which advocate for the protection of all individuals, regardless of sexual orientation or gender identity.

## Case Studies and Examples

Several documented cases highlight the dangers faced by LGBTQ individuals under the current legal framework. For instance, in 2018, a group of men was arrested in Yangon during a police raid on a private gathering. They were charged under Section 377, and the case garnered international attention, prompting protests from LGBTQ activists and allies. Such incidents illustrate the ongoing risks faced by LGBTQ individuals in Myanmar, as well as the urgent need for legal reform.

## Challenges to Decriminalization

Efforts to decriminalize homosexuality in Myanmar face significant challenges. The deeply entrenched cultural attitudes towards homosexuality, combined with political resistance, make it difficult to advocate for legal change. Many lawmakers view the issue as a moral one, influenced by conservative religious beliefs that condemn homosexuality. Additionally, the political landscape in Myanmar, characterized by military influence and instability, complicates the advocacy efforts for LGBTQ rights.

## Conclusion

In conclusion, the criminalization of homosexuality in Myanmar is a multifaceted issue that reflects historical injustices, cultural norms, and legal barriers. The implications for LGBTQ individuals are profound, affecting their safety, mental health, and ability to live authentically. Advocacy for the repeal of discriminatory laws is crucial, not only for the well-being of LGBTQ individuals but also for the broader advancement of human rights in Myanmar. As activists like Wai Wai Nu continue to fight for change, the path to decriminalization remains fraught with challenges but is essential for fostering a more inclusive society.

## Advocating for Legal Reforms

Advocating for legal reforms in Myanmar has been a pivotal aspect of the LGBTQ rights movement. The existing legal framework, which criminalizes homosexuality and perpetuates discrimination, poses significant challenges to the LGBTQ community. This section outlines the theoretical foundations of legal advocacy, the specific problems faced by LGBTQ individuals under current laws, and examples of successful reform efforts.

### Theoretical Foundations of Legal Advocacy

Legal advocacy for LGBTQ rights is grounded in several key theories, including human rights theory, social justice theory, and intersectionality. Human rights theory posits that all individuals possess inherent rights that must be protected by law. This perspective underlines the importance of legal reforms to safeguard the dignity and rights of LGBTQ individuals.

Social justice theory emphasizes the need to address systemic inequalities and injustices. Legal reforms are essential to dismantle discriminatory practices and ensure equitable treatment for all members of society. Furthermore, intersectionality highlights how various social identities—such as race, gender, and sexual orientation—interact to create unique experiences of oppression. Advocating for legal reforms requires an understanding of these intersections to effectively address the needs of marginalized groups within the LGBTQ community.

## Problems Faced by LGBTQ Individuals

The legal landscape in Myanmar is fraught with challenges for LGBTQ individuals. The Penal Code Section 377 criminalizes same-sex relationships, leading to widespread discrimination and violence. This legal framework not only perpetuates stigma but also discourages individuals from seeking justice when faced with violence or discrimination.

Moreover, the lack of legal recognition for same-sex relationships prevents LGBTQ individuals from accessing essential services, such as healthcare and housing. This legal invisibility exacerbates social isolation and economic vulnerability, making it imperative to advocate for comprehensive legal reforms that recognize and protect LGBTQ rights.

## Examples of Advocacy Efforts

Several advocacy efforts have emerged in Myanmar to challenge discriminatory laws and promote legal reforms. One notable example is the collaboration between local LGBTQ organizations and international human rights groups. These partnerships have facilitated the sharing of resources, expertise, and strategies to advocate for legal changes.

In 2019, a coalition of LGBTQ activists, supported by international NGOs, organized a campaign to lobby the Myanmar government for the repeal of Section 377. This campaign included public awareness initiatives, legal workshops, and direct engagement with policymakers. The coalition emphasized the need for legal reforms not only from a human rights perspective but also as a means to enhance public health and safety.

Another significant effort involved the documentation of human rights violations against LGBTQ individuals. By collecting testimonies and evidence of discrimination, activists were able to present a compelling case for legal reforms to both national and international bodies. This documentation served as a powerful tool to raise awareness and garner support for the repeal of oppressive laws.

## Challenges in Legal Advocacy

Despite these efforts, advocating for legal reforms in Myanmar remains fraught with challenges. The political landscape is volatile, and the government often views LGBTQ rights as a threat to traditional values. Activists face harassment, intimidation, and legal repercussions for their work, which can deter individuals from participating in advocacy efforts.

Furthermore, the deeply rooted cultural and religious beliefs surrounding sexuality and gender identity create significant barriers to acceptance and reform. Many individuals within the society hold conservative views that oppose LGBTQ rights, making it essential for advocates to engage in continuous dialogue and education to shift public perceptions.

## Conclusion

Advocating for legal reforms in Myanmar is a complex and ongoing process that requires resilience, collaboration, and strategic planning. By addressing the theoretical foundations of legal advocacy, recognizing the specific problems faced by LGBTQ individuals, and learning from successful examples, activists can continue to push for meaningful change. The journey toward legal equality is fraught with challenges, but the commitment to fighting for justice and human rights remains unwavering.

# Challenging Discriminatory Laws in Court

The legal landscape for LGBTQ individuals in Myanmar is fraught with challenges, as many laws perpetuate discrimination and violate basic human rights. One of the most pressing issues is the criminalization of homosexuality, which is enshrined in Section 377 of the Penal Code. This section, a remnant of colonial-era legislation, criminalizes consensual same-sex relationships, subjecting individuals to severe penalties, including imprisonment. To dismantle these discriminatory laws, activists like Wai Wai Nu have strategically focused on challenging such statutes in court, aiming not only to achieve legal reforms but also to shift societal perceptions regarding LGBTQ rights.

## Legal Framework and Strategies

Challenging discriminatory laws requires a multifaceted approach. Activists often begin by gathering evidence of the negative impacts of these laws on LGBTQ individuals. This evidence can include testimonies from affected individuals, statistical data on arrests and prosecutions, and expert opinions from human rights organizations. The goal is to construct a compelling case that demonstrates the laws' violation of constitutional rights, such as the right to equality, privacy, and freedom from discrimination.

A critical aspect of this strategy is the engagement of human rights lawyers who specialize in LGBTQ issues. These legal experts can navigate the complexities of the judicial system and represent activists in court. For example, in a landmark case, a group of LGBTQ activists, with the support of a human rights organization, filed a petition challenging the constitutionality of Section 377. The petition argued that the law not only infringed upon individual rights but also fostered a culture of fear and discrimination against LGBTQ individuals.

## Judicial Outcomes and Their Implications

The outcomes of such legal challenges can vary significantly. In some cases, courts may rule in favor of the petitioners, declaring the laws unconstitutional and paving the way for legal reforms. For instance, in a neighboring country, a similar legal challenge led to the decriminalization of homosexuality, marking a significant victory for LGBTQ activists. This outcome not only provided legal protection for LGBTQ individuals but also encouraged further activism and advocacy for comprehensive anti-discrimination laws.

Conversely, there are instances where courts uphold discriminatory laws, citing cultural norms or public morality as justifications. Such rulings can have a chilling effect on activism, as they reinforce societal prejudices and discourage individuals from coming forward to challenge injustices. In Myanmar, the judiciary's reluctance to confront deeply entrenched societal norms poses a significant barrier to progress.

## International Support and Solidarity

The fight against discriminatory laws is not confined to national borders. International support plays a crucial role in amplifying the voices of local activists and applying pressure on governments to reform unjust laws. Organizations such as Human Rights Watch and Amnesty International have documented human rights abuses against LGBTQ individuals in Myanmar and have called for the repeal of discriminatory laws. Their reports serve as valuable resources for activists in court, providing a broader context for their claims.

Moreover, international solidarity can take the form of strategic litigation, where cases are brought before international human rights bodies. For example, activists may appeal to the United Nations Human Rights Committee, arguing that Myanmar's laws violate international human rights treaties to which the country is a signatory. Such actions not only bring global attention to local issues but also create avenues for accountability.

## Challenges and Future Directions

Despite these efforts, challenging discriminatory laws in court remains a daunting task. Activists face numerous obstacles, including limited access to legal resources, societal stigma, and the potential for backlash from authorities. Additionally, the political climate in Myanmar, characterized by military rule and repression of dissent, complicates the pursuit of justice.

Moving forward, it is essential for LGBTQ activists to continue building coalitions with other marginalized groups and human rights organizations. By framing the struggle for LGBTQ rights as part of a broader human rights agenda, activists can foster a more inclusive movement that challenges not only discriminatory laws but also the systemic injustices faced by various communities.

In conclusion, while the path to challenging discriminatory laws in Myanmar is fraught with challenges, it is a crucial component of the broader fight for LGBTQ rights. Through strategic legal action, international support, and grassroots mobilization, activists like Wai Wai Nu are paving the way for a more just and equitable society, one court case at a time.

# Collaborating with Human Rights Lawyers

The collaboration between LGBTQ activists and human rights lawyers is pivotal in the struggle for legal reform and the protection of rights in Myanmar. This partnership not only enhances the legal framework for LGBTQ rights but also empowers activists to navigate the complex legal landscape of a country where discrimination is deeply entrenched.

## The Role of Human Rights Lawyers

Human rights lawyers play a crucial role in advocating for marginalized communities, including LGBTQ individuals. They possess the legal expertise necessary to challenge discriminatory laws and practices, and their involvement can significantly amplify the impact of activism. In Myanmar, where laws criminalizing homosexuality exist, the work of these lawyers is essential for:

+ **Legal Representation:** Providing legal defense for individuals facing charges related to their sexual orientation or gender identity.

- **Litigation:** Challenging unjust laws in court to set legal precedents that protect LGBTQ rights.

- **Advisory Services:** Offering guidance on legal rights and the implications of existing laws for LGBTQ individuals and activists.

## Challenges Faced in Collaboration

Despite the potential benefits, several challenges arise in the collaboration between LGBTQ activists and human rights lawyers in Myanmar:

- **Limited Legal Framework:** The existing legal framework often lacks protections for LGBTQ individuals, making it difficult for lawyers to argue cases effectively. The criminalization of homosexuality under Section 377 of the Penal Code presents a significant barrier.

- **Risk of Retaliation:** Lawyers who take on LGBTQ cases may face backlash from the state or society, including harassment, threats, or even legal repercussions. This risk can deter legal professionals from engaging with LGBTQ issues.

- **Resource Constraints:** Many human rights lawyers operate within NGOs that may have limited resources, affecting their capacity to take on multiple cases or provide extensive support to LGBTQ activists.

- **Cultural Stigma:** Cultural attitudes towards homosexuality can create an environment of fear, making it challenging for lawyers to advocate openly for LGBTQ rights without facing social ostracism.

## Successful Collaborations: Case Studies

Despite these challenges, there have been notable examples of successful collaborations between LGBTQ activists and human rights lawyers in Myanmar:

- **The Case of John Doe:** A landmark case where a young man was arrested under Section 377. A team of human rights lawyers worked with LGBTQ activists to mount a robust defense, arguing that the law violated international human rights standards. The case garnered significant media attention, highlighting the need for legal reform.

- **Legal Workshops:** Human rights lawyers have conducted workshops in collaboration with LGBTQ organizations to educate activists about their legal rights and the judicial process. These workshops empower activists to advocate for themselves and their communities more effectively.

- **Joint Advocacy Campaigns:** Activists and lawyers have joined forces to lobby for legal reforms at both local and international levels, presenting a united front that emphasizes the importance of LGBTQ rights in the broader context of human rights.

## Theoretical Framework: Intersectionality in Legal Advocacy

The collaboration between LGBTQ activists and human rights lawyers can be analyzed through the lens of intersectionality, a theory that examines how various social identities (such as race, gender, and sexual orientation) intersect to create unique experiences of discrimination and privilege.

In the context of Myanmar, intersectionality reveals how LGBTQ individuals, particularly those from ethnic minority backgrounds, face compounded discrimination. Human rights lawyers who understand this framework can tailor their legal strategies to address the specific needs of these individuals, advocating for more inclusive policies that recognize the complexity of their experiences.

## Future Directions for Collaboration

Moving forward, it is crucial for LGBTQ activists and human rights lawyers to strengthen their collaboration through:

- **Building Trust:** Establishing a rapport between activists and lawyers to ensure open communication and mutual understanding of goals.

- **Expanding Networks:** Engaging with international human rights organizations to share knowledge, resources, and strategies that can enhance local efforts.

- **Advocating for Legal Reforms:** Jointly pushing for legislative changes that decriminalize homosexuality and protect LGBTQ rights, thereby creating a more inclusive legal environment.

- **Increasing Visibility:** Utilizing media platforms to raise awareness about the legal challenges faced by LGBTQ individuals, thus garnering public support and putting pressure on policymakers.

In conclusion, the collaboration between LGBTQ activists and human rights lawyers is a vital component of the fight for equality in Myanmar. By leveraging their respective strengths, they can create a more just and equitable society for all individuals, regardless of their sexual orientation or gender identity. The continued partnership between these two groups will be instrumental in overcoming the legal and social barriers that persist in Myanmar today.

## Lobbying for Legislative Changes

Lobbying for legislative changes is a crucial component of the LGBTQ rights movement in Myanmar. It involves strategically influencing policymakers to enact laws that protect the rights of LGBTQ individuals and dismantle discriminatory practices. This section explores the theoretical framework behind lobbying, the challenges faced, and successful examples of advocacy within the context of Myanmar.

### Theoretical Framework

The theory of advocacy and lobbying is grounded in several key principles. First, it is essential to understand the political landscape and the mechanisms through which laws are created and amended. Advocacy often involves building coalitions, mobilizing public opinion, and directly engaging with legislators. The **Advocacy Coalition Framework** (ACF) posits that policy change occurs when coalitions of actors with shared beliefs work together over time to influence public policy. In the context of LGBTQ rights, this means uniting various stakeholders, including activists, legal experts, and sympathetic politicians, to create a cohesive front for change.

$$C = \{A_1, A_2, \ldots, A_n\} \tag{23}$$

Where $C$ is the coalition and $A_i$ represents the individual actors involved in the advocacy efforts.

### Challenges in Lobbying

Lobbying for LGBTQ legislative changes in Myanmar is fraught with challenges. The political environment is often hostile, and LGBTQ individuals face significant discrimination and stigma. Key challenges include:

+ **Legal Barriers:** Homosexuality remains criminalized under Section 377 of the Myanmar Penal Code, creating a legal framework that is inherently biased against LGBTQ individuals. This legal status complicates efforts to advocate for rights and protections.

+ **Cultural Resistance:** Deep-rooted cultural norms and religious beliefs contribute to widespread homophobia and transphobia, making it difficult to gain public support for legislative changes.

+ **Limited Resources:** Many LGBTQ organizations operate on limited budgets and rely on external funding, which can hinder sustained lobbying efforts.

+ **Fear of Repercussions:** Activists often face threats, harassment, and violence, which can deter them from engaging in lobbying activities.

## Strategies for Effective Lobbying

To overcome these challenges, LGBTQ activists in Myanmar have employed various strategies to lobby for legislative changes effectively:

1. **Building Alliances:** Forming alliances with human rights organizations, legal experts, and sympathetic political figures has been vital. These partnerships enhance credibility and provide access to necessary resources.

2. **Public Awareness Campaigns:** Raising awareness about LGBTQ issues through media campaigns, public demonstrations, and educational workshops helps shift public opinion and garner support for legislative reforms.

3. **Direct Engagement with Policymakers:** Organizing meetings with lawmakers, presenting research, and sharing personal stories are essential tactics to humanize the issues and persuade legislators to act.

4. **Utilizing International Support:** Engaging with international human rights organizations and leveraging global attention can pressure the Myanmar government to consider legislative changes.

## Successful Examples

Despite the challenges, there have been notable successes in lobbying for LGBTQ rights in Myanmar:

+ **The 2019 LGBTQ Rights Conference:** This event brought together activists, legal experts, and policymakers to discuss the need for legal reforms. The conference resulted in a joint statement advocating for the decriminalization of homosexuality and the establishment of anti-discrimination laws.

+ **Collaborative Legal Efforts:** LGBTQ activists collaborated with human rights lawyers to challenge discriminatory laws in court. These legal battles have raised awareness and highlighted the need for legislative change.

+ **International Advocacy:** Activists successfully engaged with international bodies such as the United Nations, which has pressured the Myanmar government to address human rights violations against LGBTQ individuals.

### Conclusion

Lobbying for legislative changes is a complex but necessary endeavor in the fight for LGBTQ rights in Myanmar. By understanding the theoretical framework, recognizing the challenges, and employing effective strategies, activists can create a powerful movement for change. The journey towards equality is fraught with obstacles, but the resilience and determination of LGBTQ activists continue to pave the way for a more inclusive and just society.

$$R = \sum_{i=1}^{n}(C_i \cdot E_i) \tag{24}$$

Where $R$ represents the overall impact of lobbying efforts, $C_i$ is the coalition strength, and $E_i$ is the effectiveness of each strategy employed.

Through persistent advocacy and strategic lobbying, the dream of a society where LGBTQ individuals can live freely and authentically in Myanmar is gradually becoming a reality.

# Strengthening Healthcare and Support Systems

## Addressing LGBTQ-Specific Health Needs

The health needs of LGBTQ individuals in Myanmar are often overlooked due to pervasive societal stigma, discrimination, and inadequate healthcare services. Addressing these specific health needs is essential for promoting the well-being of LGBTQ communities and ensuring equitable access to healthcare.

## Understanding Health Disparities

LGBTQ individuals frequently face unique health disparities compared to their heterosexual counterparts. These disparities can be attributed to a variety of factors, including:

- **Social Stigma:** The stigma associated with being LGBTQ can lead to mental health challenges, including anxiety, depression, and suicidal ideation. Research indicates that LGBTQ youth are significantly more likely to experience mental health issues than their heterosexual peers [1].

- **Discrimination in Healthcare:** Many LGBTQ individuals encounter discrimination when seeking medical care, which can result in avoidance of healthcare services altogether. A study by the National Center for Transgender Equality found that 19% of transgender individuals reported being refused care due to their gender identity [2].

- **Lack of Cultural Competence:** Healthcare providers may lack the training necessary to understand and address the specific health needs of LGBTQ patients, leading to inadequate care. This can include a lack of understanding regarding sexual health, mental health, and the unique challenges faced by LGBTQ individuals.

## Key Health Needs

To effectively address the health needs of LGBTQ individuals, it is crucial to focus on several key areas:

- **Mental Health Services:** Given the high rates of mental health issues within LGBTQ populations, it is imperative to provide accessible mental health resources. This includes counseling services that are affirming and culturally competent. Programs should be developed that specifically target the needs of LGBTQ youth, who are particularly vulnerable to mental health challenges.

- **Sexual Health Services:** Access to sexual health services, including STI testing and treatment, is essential. LGBTQ individuals should be educated on safe sex practices and have access to preventive measures such as PrEP (pre-exposure prophylaxis) to reduce the risk of HIV transmission.

* **Substance Abuse Support:** LGBTQ individuals are at a higher risk of substance abuse due to the stressors associated with discrimination and stigma. Support groups and rehabilitation programs tailored to LGBTQ individuals can help address these issues in a safe and supportive environment.

* **Transgender Healthcare:** Transgender individuals face unique healthcare challenges, including access to hormone therapy and gender-affirming surgeries. It is vital for healthcare providers to understand the specific needs of transgender patients and provide comprehensive care that respects their gender identity.

## Implementing Solutions

To effectively address these health needs, several strategies can be employed:

* **Training Healthcare Providers:** Developing training programs for healthcare professionals to increase their cultural competence regarding LGBTQ health issues is essential. This training should encompass topics such as understanding gender identity, sexual orientation, and the specific health risks faced by LGBTQ individuals.

* **Creating Inclusive Policies:** Healthcare institutions should implement policies that explicitly prohibit discrimination against LGBTQ patients. These policies should be enforced through regular training and evaluation of staff practices.

* **Community Outreach:** Engaging with LGBTQ communities through outreach programs can help raise awareness about available health services. Collaborating with local LGBTQ organizations can facilitate trust and encourage individuals to seek the care they need.

* **Advocacy for Legal Protections:** Advocating for legal protections for LGBTQ individuals in healthcare settings is crucial. This includes lobbying for laws that prohibit discrimination based on sexual orientation and gender identity in all aspects of healthcare.

## Examples of Successful Initiatives

Several initiatives have successfully addressed LGBTQ-specific health needs in various contexts:

+ **The Rainbow Health Ontario Initiative:** This program provides training to healthcare providers on LGBTQ health issues and promotes inclusive practices in healthcare settings. It has successfully increased the number of LGBTQ individuals accessing health services in Ontario, Canada [3].

+ **The Transgender Health Program in San Francisco:** This program offers comprehensive healthcare services tailored to the needs of transgender individuals, including hormone therapy and mental health support. It serves as a model for providing affirming care to transgender patients [4].

## Conclusion

Addressing LGBTQ-specific health needs in Myanmar is a critical component of advancing health equity and promoting the well-being of marginalized communities. By understanding the unique health challenges faced by LGBTQ individuals and implementing targeted solutions, healthcare providers can create a more inclusive and supportive healthcare environment. This will not only improve health outcomes for LGBTQ individuals but also contribute to the broader movement for LGBTQ rights and acceptance in society.

# Bibliography

[1] Meyer, I. H. (2003). Prejudice, Social Stress, and Mental Health in Gay Men. *American Psychologist*, 58(5), 123-134.

[2] National Center for Transgender Equality (2015). *The Report of the 2015 U.S. Transgender Survey*.

[3] Rainbow Health Ontario (2016). *Improving Health Care for LGBTQ Communities: A Guide for Health Care Providers*.

[4] San Francisco Department of Public Health (2018). *Transgender Health Program: Comprehensive Healthcare for Transgender Individuals*.

## Promoting LGBTQ-Inclusive Healthcare Services

In Myanmar, the promotion of LGBTQ-inclusive healthcare services is a critical aspect of advancing the rights and well-being of LGBTQ individuals. This initiative not only addresses the unique health needs of the LGBTQ community but also seeks to dismantle the systemic barriers that have historically marginalized these populations within the healthcare system.

## Understanding LGBTQ Health Needs

The healthcare needs of LGBTQ individuals are diverse and often differ significantly from those of their heterosexual counterparts. Key areas of concern include:

- **Mental Health:** LGBTQ individuals frequently experience higher rates of mental health issues, such as depression and anxiety, often stemming from societal stigma, discrimination, and isolation. According to the *National Institute of Mental Health*, LGBTQ youth are at a greater risk for suicidal ideation compared to their heterosexual peers.

+ **Sexual Health:** Access to sexual health services, including STI testing and treatment, is essential. LGBTQ individuals may face barriers in obtaining these services due to fear of discrimination or lack of knowledge among healthcare providers about LGBTQ-specific health issues.

+ **Substance Use:** Higher rates of substance use and abuse have been documented in the LGBTQ community, often linked to stressors related to discrimination and social marginalization.

+ **Transgender Healthcare:** Transgender individuals require specific healthcare services, including hormone therapy and gender-affirming surgeries, which are often inaccessible in conservative healthcare settings.

## Barriers to Accessing Healthcare

Several barriers hinder LGBTQ individuals from accessing adequate healthcare services in Myanmar:

+ **Discrimination and Stigma:** Many LGBTQ individuals encounter discriminatory practices within healthcare settings, leading to reluctance to seek care.

+ **Lack of Training:** Healthcare providers often lack training on LGBTQ health issues, resulting in inadequate care and misunderstandings about the needs of LGBTQ patients.

+ **Legal and Policy Constraints:** The criminalization of homosexuality in Myanmar creates an environment of fear, discouraging individuals from seeking necessary healthcare services.

## Strategies for Promoting LGBTQ-Inclusive Healthcare

To effectively promote LGBTQ-inclusive healthcare services, several strategies can be implemented:

+ **Training Healthcare Providers:** Implementing comprehensive training programs for healthcare professionals is essential. These programs should cover LGBTQ health issues, cultural competency, and strategies for creating a welcoming environment for LGBTQ patients.

+ **Creating Safe Spaces:** Establishing healthcare facilities that explicitly identify as LGBTQ-friendly can help create a safe environment for patients. This may involve signage, inclusive language in patient forms, and staff trained in LGBTQ sensitivity.

+ **Advocating for Policy Changes:** Collaborating with local and international NGOs to advocate for legal reforms that protect LGBTQ individuals from discrimination in healthcare settings is crucial. This includes lobbying for the decriminalization of homosexuality and the establishment of non-discriminatory healthcare policies.

+ **Community Engagement and Outreach:** Engaging with LGBTQ communities to understand their specific health needs and concerns can guide the development of targeted healthcare programs. Outreach initiatives can help raise awareness about available services and encourage individuals to seek care.

+ **Developing Educational Resources:** Creating educational materials that inform LGBTQ individuals about their health rights and available healthcare services can empower them to advocate for their needs.

## Examples of Successful Initiatives

Several successful initiatives worldwide can serve as models for promoting LGBTQ-inclusive healthcare services in Myanmar:

+ **The Rainbow Health Ontario:** This program provides training for healthcare providers in Ontario, Canada, emphasizing the importance of inclusive practices. It has led to increased confidence among providers in delivering care to LGBTQ patients.

+ **The Transgender Health Program in San Francisco:** This program offers comprehensive healthcare services tailored to the needs of transgender individuals, including mental health support and hormone therapy. It has become a model for other cities seeking to improve transgender healthcare access.

## Conclusion

Promoting LGBTQ-inclusive healthcare services is essential for improving health outcomes and ensuring equitable access to care for LGBTQ individuals in

Myanmar. By addressing the unique health needs of this community, dismantling barriers to access, and implementing effective strategies, we can foster a more inclusive healthcare system that respects and affirms the dignity of all individuals, regardless of their sexual orientation or gender identity. The journey towards inclusive healthcare is not just a matter of health; it is a fundamental human right that must be championed by all sectors of society.

## Mental Health Support for LGBTQ Individuals

The mental health of LGBTQ individuals is a critical concern, particularly in societies where stigma, discrimination, and violence against sexual and gender minorities are prevalent. Research indicates that LGBTQ individuals are at a higher risk for mental health issues such as depression, anxiety, and suicidal ideation compared to their heterosexual and cisgender counterparts [1]. This increased vulnerability can be attributed to a variety of factors, including societal rejection, internalized homophobia, and lack of access to affirmative healthcare.

### Understanding the Issues

Several theoretical frameworks can help us understand the mental health challenges faced by LGBTQ individuals. One prominent theory is the *Minority Stress Theory*, which posits that the unique stressors experienced by minority groups, including stigma, discrimination, and social isolation, contribute to higher rates of mental health issues [1]. These stressors can be categorized into three types:

- **External Stressors:** These include societal discrimination, harassment, and violence directed at LGBTQ individuals. For example, a study by [2] found that LGBTQ individuals who experienced discrimination were more likely to report symptoms of depression and anxiety.

- **Internalized Stressors:** These arise from the internalization of societal stigma, leading individuals to feel shame or self-hatred regarding their sexual orientation or gender identity. For instance, many LGBTQ youth may struggle with self-acceptance, leading to feelings of worthlessness and isolation.

- **Expectancy Stressors:** These are the anticipatory fears of rejection or discrimination that LGBTQ individuals may experience in various settings, such as workplaces or family gatherings. This constant vigilance can lead to heightened anxiety and stress.

The cumulative effect of these stressors can result in a range of mental health challenges, including increased rates of depression, anxiety disorders, and suicidal ideation. According to the *National Alliance on Mental Illness (NAMI)*, LGBTQ individuals are more than twice as likely to experience a mental health condition compared to heterosexual individuals [3].

## Barriers to Mental Health Support

Despite the pressing need for mental health support, many LGBTQ individuals face significant barriers to accessing care. These barriers can include:

+ **Stigma within the Healthcare System:** Many LGBTQ individuals report experiencing discrimination or bias from healthcare providers, which can deter them from seeking help [2].

+ **Lack of LGBTQ-Competent Providers:** There is a shortage of mental health professionals who are trained to understand and address the unique needs of LGBTQ clients. This lack of competency can lead to inadequate treatment and further marginalization of LGBTQ individuals [1].

+ **Financial Constraints:** Economic disparities within the LGBTQ community, particularly among marginalized groups, can limit access to mental health services. Many LGBTQ individuals may lack insurance coverage or the financial means to afford therapy [3].

## Promoting Mental Health Support

To address these challenges, it is essential to develop and promote mental health support systems that are inclusive and affirming of LGBTQ identities. Some strategies include:

+ **Training for Mental Health Professionals:** Providing training programs for mental health professionals on LGBTQ issues can help reduce bias and improve the quality of care. This training should encompass cultural competency, understanding of gender identity, and the specific mental health needs of LGBTQ individuals.

+ **Creating Safe Spaces:** Establishing LGBTQ-specific support groups and community centers can provide a safe and affirming environment for individuals to share their experiences and seek help. These spaces can facilitate peer support, which has been shown to improve mental health outcomes [2].

+ **Advocacy for Policy Change:** Engaging in advocacy efforts to promote LGBTQ-inclusive mental health policies can help improve access to care. This includes lobbying for insurance coverage for mental health services and ensuring that mental health resources are available in schools and community organizations.

+ **Utilizing Technology:** Teletherapy and online support groups can provide accessible mental health resources for LGBTQ individuals, particularly those in rural or underserved areas. This approach can help overcome geographical barriers and provide support in a comfortable setting [3].

## Conclusion

In conclusion, mental health support for LGBTQ individuals is a vital component of promoting overall well-being and resilience within this community. By addressing the unique challenges faced by LGBTQ individuals and advocating for inclusive mental health resources, we can create a more supportive environment that fosters acceptance, understanding, and healing. As we move forward, it is crucial to remember that mental health is an integral part of human rights, and every individual deserves access to the care and support they need to thrive.

# Bibliography

[1] Meyer, I. H. (2003). Prejudice, Social Stress, and Mental Health in Gay Men. *American Psychologist*, 58(5), 1-14.

[2] Budge, S. L., Adelson, J. L., & Howard, K. A. (2013). Anxiety and Depression in Transgender Individuals: The Roles of Social Support and Social Identity. *Journal of Consulting and Clinical Psychology*, 81(3), 545-557.

[3] National Alliance on Mental Illness. (2021). LGBTQ+ Mental Health. Retrieved from https://www.nami.org

## Building a Network of LGBTQ Support Groups

The establishment of a robust network of LGBTQ support groups is fundamental to creating a safe and nurturing environment for LGBTQ individuals in Myanmar. This network not only provides emotional and psychological support but also fosters a sense of community and belonging among its members. The importance of support groups cannot be overstated, as they play a crucial role in combating isolation, stigma, and discrimination that LGBTQ individuals often face in traditional societies.

### Theoretical Framework

Support groups operate under several psychological and sociological theories. One prominent theory is the *Social Support Theory*, which posits that individuals who perceive themselves as being supported by others are more likely to experience positive mental health outcomes. According to Cohen and Wills (1985), social support can be categorized into three types: emotional support, informational support, and tangible support. Each of these types is vital for LGBTQ individuals, who may experience unique stressors related to their sexual orientation and gender identity.

Furthermore, the *Minority Stress Theory* developed by Meyer (2003) highlights the chronic stress faced by marginalized groups, including LGBTQ individuals. This theory suggests that the stigma and discrimination associated with being part of a minority group can lead to mental health challenges. Support groups can mitigate these effects by providing a safe space for individuals to share their experiences and receive validation.

## Challenges in Building Support Groups

Despite the clear benefits, establishing LGBTQ support groups in Myanmar presents several challenges:

+ **Cultural Stigma:** The deeply rooted cultural norms and values in Myanmar often lead to the stigmatization of LGBTQ individuals. This stigma can deter individuals from seeking help or participating in support groups, as they may fear judgment or discrimination.

+ **Legal Barriers:** Homosexuality is criminalized in Myanmar, creating an environment of fear and secrecy. This legal context complicates the formation of visible support groups, as participants may worry about legal repercussions.

+ **Resource Limitations:** Many LGBTQ organizations in Myanmar operate on limited funding and resources, making it difficult to establish and sustain support groups. This limitation can hinder outreach efforts and the ability to provide comprehensive services.

+ **Lack of Awareness:** There is often a lack of awareness regarding the existence and benefits of support groups among LGBTQ individuals. Without effective outreach and education, potential members may remain unaware of the resources available to them.

## Strategies for Building Support Networks

To effectively build a network of LGBTQ support groups, several strategies can be employed:

+ **Community Engagement:** Engaging with the community through outreach programs can help raise awareness about the importance of support groups. This can include informational workshops, community events, and collaborations with local organizations that align with LGBTQ rights.

+ **Creating Safe Spaces:** Establishing safe and confidential spaces for group meetings is crucial. These spaces should be accessible and welcoming to all members, allowing individuals to share their experiences without fear of judgment.

+ **Training Facilitators:** Providing training for group facilitators on LGBTQ issues, mental health, and effective communication can enhance the quality of support offered. Trained facilitators can create an environment that fosters trust and openness among participants.

+ **Utilizing Technology:** In a country where physical meetings may pose risks, leveraging technology can be a powerful tool. Online support groups and forums can provide anonymity and accessibility, allowing individuals to connect without geographical or legal constraints.

+ **Building Alliances:** Collaborating with existing NGOs, human rights organizations, and healthcare providers can strengthen support networks. These partnerships can provide additional resources, expertise, and legitimacy to LGBTQ support initiatives.

## Examples of Successful Support Groups

Several examples of successful LGBTQ support groups can serve as models for initiatives in Myanmar:

+ **The Rainbow Support Group in Thailand:** This group provides emotional support, legal assistance, and health services to LGBTQ individuals. Its success lies in its inclusive approach and collaboration with local healthcare providers.

+ **The Queer Youth Network in the Philippines:** This organization focuses on empowering LGBTQ youth through peer support and advocacy. Their use of social media to reach a broader audience has proven effective in engaging young individuals.

+ **The Black LGBTQ+ Migrant Project in the U.S.:** This project highlights the intersectionality of race and sexual orientation. It provides support to LGBTQ migrants, emphasizing the importance of addressing multiple layers of identity within support networks.

## Conclusion

Building a network of LGBTQ support groups in Myanmar is a vital step toward fostering acceptance and understanding within society. By addressing the unique challenges faced by LGBTQ individuals and employing effective strategies, these support networks can provide essential resources and community for those in need. The journey towards equality and acceptance is ongoing, but with perseverance and solidarity, LGBTQ individuals in Myanmar can find strength in their shared experiences and build a brighter future together.

# The Role of Medical Professionals in Advocacy

In the ongoing struggle for LGBTQ rights in Myanmar, the involvement of medical professionals is crucial. Their unique position allows them to address health disparities, advocate for inclusive policies, and challenge the stigma surrounding LGBTQ individuals. This section explores the vital role of healthcare providers in promoting LGBTQ rights and fostering an environment of acceptance and understanding.

## Understanding Health Disparities

LGBTQ individuals often face significant health disparities compared to their heterosexual counterparts. These disparities can arise from a lack of access to appropriate healthcare services, discrimination within healthcare settings, and the psychological impacts of societal stigma. Medical professionals have the responsibility to recognize these disparities and work towards mitigating them.

For instance, studies have shown that LGBTQ individuals are at a higher risk for mental health issues, including depression and anxiety, often stemming from societal rejection and discrimination [1]. Medical professionals can advocate for mental health resources tailored specifically for LGBTQ patients, ensuring they receive the support they need.

## Advocating for Inclusive Healthcare Policies

Medical professionals can play a pivotal role in advocating for inclusive healthcare policies that protect the rights of LGBTQ individuals. This advocacy can take many forms, from lobbying for non-discrimination policies in healthcare facilities to promoting LGBTQ-inclusive training for healthcare providers.

For example, the American Medical Association (AMA) has established policies that support the inclusion of LGBTQ health issues in medical education and practice. By aligning with such initiatives, Myanmar's healthcare professionals can help create a more equitable healthcare system. This includes pushing for policies that ensure all individuals, regardless of their sexual orientation or gender identity, have access to comprehensive healthcare services.

## Training and Education

Education is a powerful tool in combating prejudice and misinformation. Medical professionals must receive training that includes LGBTQ health issues and cultural competency. This training helps providers understand the unique needs of LGBTQ patients and fosters an environment of trust and safety.

In Myanmar, initiatives such as workshops and seminars aimed at healthcare professionals can be instrumental in raising awareness about LGBTQ health concerns. For instance, organizations can collaborate with medical schools to integrate LGBTQ health topics into their curricula, ensuring that future healthcare providers are well-equipped to serve diverse populations.

## Creating Safe Spaces within Healthcare Settings

Creating safe spaces for LGBTQ individuals within healthcare settings is essential. Medical professionals can advocate for policies that protect LGBTQ patients from discrimination and harassment. This involves training staff to be sensitive to the needs of LGBTQ patients and ensuring that facilities are welcoming and inclusive.

An example of this can be seen in the establishment of LGBTQ-friendly clinics that specifically cater to the needs of this community. These clinics can provide a range of services, including mental health support, sexual health services, and general medical care, all in a safe and affirming environment.

## Research and Data Collection

Medical professionals can contribute to the body of knowledge surrounding LGBTQ health issues by engaging in research and data collection. Understanding the specific health needs of LGBTQ individuals in Myanmar is crucial for developing effective interventions and policies.

For instance, conducting surveys and studies that focus on LGBTQ health can provide valuable insights into the challenges faced by this community. This data can then be used to advocate for necessary changes within the healthcare system, ensuring that LGBTQ individuals receive the care they deserve.

### Collaborating with LGBTQ Organizations

Collaboration between medical professionals and LGBTQ organizations can enhance advocacy efforts and improve health outcomes for LGBTQ individuals. By working together, healthcare providers and activists can address systemic barriers and promote policies that protect LGBTQ rights.

For example, partnerships can be formed to organize health fairs, provide free health screenings, and disseminate information about LGBTQ health issues. These collaborative efforts can help bridge the gap between healthcare providers and the LGBTQ community, fostering trust and improving access to care.

### Conclusion

The role of medical professionals in advocating for LGBTQ rights in Myanmar is multifaceted and essential. By recognizing health disparities, advocating for inclusive policies, providing education, creating safe spaces, engaging in research, and collaborating with LGBTQ organizations, healthcare providers can significantly impact the lives of LGBTQ individuals. Their commitment to advocacy not only improves health outcomes but also contributes to the broader movement for equality and acceptance within society.

# Creating Safe Spaces

## Establishing LGBTQ Community Centers

Establishing LGBTQ community centers is a critical step towards fostering a safe, inclusive, and supportive environment for LGBTQ individuals in Myanmar. These centers serve as vital hubs for community engagement, education, and advocacy, addressing the unique challenges faced by LGBTQ individuals in a predominantly conservative society.

### The Role of Community Centers

Community centers play a multifaceted role in the LGBTQ rights movement. They provide a space for social interaction, education, and support, which is essential for individuals who may feel isolated due to their sexual orientation or gender identity. As highlighted by [?], community centers can help mitigate the negative effects of social stigma by creating a sense of belonging and solidarity among LGBTQ individuals.

## Challenges in Establishing Centers

Despite their importance, establishing LGBTQ community centers in Myanmar presents several challenges.

+ **Societal Resistance:** The conservative nature of Burmese society often leads to resistance against LGBTQ initiatives. Activists may face backlash from community members who perceive these centers as threats to traditional values.

+ **Funding and Resources:** Securing funding is another significant hurdle. Many potential donors may hesitate to support LGBTQ initiatives due to fear of social repercussions or legal implications, especially in a country where homosexuality is criminalized.

+ **Safety Concerns:** Activists and community members may face threats of violence or harassment when attempting to establish these centers. The fear of persecution can deter individuals from participating in community-building efforts.

## Best Practices for Establishing Centers

To effectively establish LGBTQ community centers, several best practices should be considered:

1. **Community Engagement:** Engaging with the local community is essential. This involves educating the public about LGBTQ issues and fostering dialogue to reduce stigma. Initiatives such as community forums or workshops can help build understanding and support.

2. **Collaborative Partnerships:** Forming partnerships with local NGOs, human rights organizations, and even sympathetic businesses can provide the necessary resources and legitimacy. Collaboration can also enhance visibility and broaden the reach of LGBTQ initiatives.

3. **Safety Protocols:** Establishing safety protocols is crucial. This includes creating a secure environment for community members and ensuring that personal information is protected. Training staff and volunteers on how to handle potential threats is also vital.

4. **Diverse Programming:** Offering a variety of programs can attract a wider audience. This may include support groups, educational workshops, cultural events, and health services tailored to the LGBTQ community. A diverse program can address the varying needs of community members and encourage participation.

5. **Advocacy and Awareness:** Community centers should also serve as platforms for advocacy. By organizing events that raise awareness about LGBTQ rights and issues, these centers can amplify the voices of marginalized individuals and push for systemic change.

## Case Studies and Examples

Several successful LGBTQ community centers around the world offer valuable lessons for Myanmar:

- **The LGBTQ Center in New York City:** This center has become a model for LGBTQ advocacy and support, offering a range of services from mental health support to legal assistance. Its success stems from strong community ties and a robust volunteer network.

- **The Rainbow Center in Washington, D.C.:** Focused on creating a safe space for LGBTQ youth, the Rainbow Center provides educational resources and mentorship programs. Its emphasis on youth engagement has proven effective in fostering a new generation of activists.

- **The Pride Center in Orlando, Florida:** This center exemplifies the importance of intersectionality in LGBTQ advocacy. By addressing the needs of diverse communities, including people of color and those with disabilities, the Pride Center has cultivated an inclusive environment that resonates with a wide audience.

## Conclusion

Establishing LGBTQ community centers in Myanmar is a challenging yet essential endeavor. By addressing societal resistance, securing funding, and ensuring safety, activists can create spaces that empower LGBTQ individuals and foster a sense of community. Drawing inspiration from successful models around the world can provide valuable insights and strategies for overcoming obstacles. Ultimately, these centers can play a pivotal role in advancing LGBTQ rights in Myanmar, creating a more inclusive society for all.

## Safe Housing for LGBTQ Individuals

The quest for safe housing is a fundamental human right, yet for LGBTQ individuals in Myanmar, it remains a pressing challenge. In a society where traditional values often clash with modern identities, many LGBTQ individuals face discrimination and violence, leading to homelessness or unsafe living conditions. This section explores the critical need for safe housing, the barriers faced by LGBTQ individuals, and potential solutions to create inclusive living environments.

## The Need for Safe Housing

Safe housing is not merely a shelter; it is a sanctuary where individuals can express their identities without fear of persecution. According to the *United Nations Housing Rights Programme*, adequate housing is essential for the well-being and dignity of all individuals. For LGBTQ individuals, the stakes are particularly high. Many are forced to leave their homes due to rejection by family members or threats of violence, resulting in a higher incidence of homelessness among LGBTQ youth.

A study conducted by the *Myanmar LGBTQ Alliance* revealed that over 30% of LGBTQ individuals had experienced homelessness at some point in their lives. This alarming statistic underscores the urgent need for safe housing solutions tailored to the unique challenges faced by the LGBTQ community.

## Barriers to Safe Housing

Several barriers hinder LGBTQ individuals from accessing safe housing in Myanmar:

- **Discrimination by Landlords:** Many landlords refuse to rent to LGBTQ tenants due to prejudices, leading to a lack of available housing options.

- **Fear of Violence:** The threat of violence from neighbors or community members often forces LGBTQ individuals to remain in unsafe living situations or seek refuge in transient accommodations, such as shelters that may not be LGBTQ-friendly.

- **Lack of Legal Protections:** The absence of anti-discrimination laws in housing exacerbates the vulnerability of LGBTQ individuals, making it difficult for them to seek legal recourse when faced with discrimination.

+ **Economic Disparities:** Many LGBTQ individuals experience economic hardships due to job discrimination, limiting their ability to afford safe housing options.

## Creating Safe Housing Solutions

To address the pressing need for safe housing, various strategies can be implemented:

+ **Establishment of LGBTQ Community Centers:** Community centers can serve as safe havens, providing temporary housing, resources, and support for LGBTQ individuals in crisis. These centers can also offer workshops on tenant rights and housing options.

+ **Partnerships with NGOs:** Collaborating with local and international non-governmental organizations (NGOs) can help secure funding and resources to create safe housing initiatives. For example, partnerships with organizations like *OutRight Action International* can facilitate the establishment of safe housing projects tailored to the needs of LGBTQ individuals.

+ **Advocacy for Legal Reforms:** Activists must lobby for the implementation of anti-discrimination laws that protect LGBTQ individuals in housing. Legal protections would empower individuals to challenge discriminatory practices and secure their right to safe living conditions.

+ **Awareness Campaigns:** Educating landlords and the general public about LGBTQ issues can help reduce stigma and promote acceptance. Campaigns that highlight the importance of diversity and inclusion in housing can foster a more welcoming environment for LGBTQ tenants.

## Case Studies and Examples

Several successful initiatives have emerged globally that can serve as models for Myanmar:

+ **The Rainbow Housing Project in Thailand:** This initiative provides safe housing for LGBTQ individuals, offering both temporary and permanent accommodations. The project emphasizes community engagement and support, creating a nurturing environment for residents.

+ **The Ali Forney Center in New York City:** This organization focuses on homeless LGBTQ youth, providing shelter, counseling, and job training. The success of this model demonstrates the importance of comprehensive support systems in addressing housing insecurity.

## Conclusion

Ensuring safe housing for LGBTQ individuals in Myanmar is a critical step toward fostering an inclusive society. By addressing the barriers to safe housing, implementing innovative solutions, and learning from successful global initiatives, Myanmar can pave the way for a future where all individuals, regardless of their sexual orientation or gender identity, can live safely and authentically. The journey toward safe housing is not just about providing shelter; it is about affirming the dignity and rights of every individual in the community.

$$\text{Safe Housing} \rightarrow \text{LGBTQ Well-Being} \rightarrow \text{Community Acceptance} \qquad (25)$$

## Promoting LGBTQ-Friendly Workplaces

The workplace is a critical environment for fostering inclusivity and acceptance of LGBTQ individuals. Promoting LGBTQ-friendly workplaces goes beyond mere tolerance; it involves creating a culture where all employees feel safe, respected, and valued regardless of their sexual orientation or gender identity. This section explores the importance of LGBTQ-friendly workplaces, the challenges faced, and strategies for fostering inclusivity.

### Importance of LGBTQ-Friendly Workplaces

Creating an LGBTQ-friendly workplace is essential for several reasons:

+ **Enhancing Employee Well-Being:** A supportive work environment significantly contributes to the mental and emotional well-being of LGBTQ employees. Studies show that employees who feel accepted are more likely to report higher job satisfaction and lower levels of stress [1].

+ **Boosting Productivity:** When employees feel safe and supported, their productivity levels increase. A 2019 study by the Human Rights Campaign found that inclusive workplaces experience a 25% increase in employee productivity [?].

+ **Attracting Talent:** Companies that promote diversity and inclusion are more appealing to potential employees. Research indicates that 70% of LGBTQ individuals consider workplace inclusivity when applying for jobs [?].

+ **Enhancing Company Reputation:** Organizations that actively promote LGBTQ rights tend to have a better public image. This positive reputation can lead to increased customer loyalty and brand strength [?].

## Challenges in Creating LGBTQ-Friendly Workplaces

Despite the benefits, many organizations face significant challenges in creating LGBTQ-friendly workplaces:

+ **Cultural Resistance:** In many societies, traditional views on gender and sexuality persist, leading to resistance against LGBTQ inclusion. Employees may fear backlash or ostracism for advocating for LGBTQ rights [?].

+ **Lack of Awareness:** Many employers and employees may lack knowledge about LGBTQ issues, leading to unintentional discrimination or microaggressions. Education and training are crucial to overcoming these barriers [?].

+ **Inadequate Policies:** Without comprehensive anti-discrimination policies that explicitly include sexual orientation and gender identity, LGBTQ employees may not have adequate protection against harassment or discrimination [?].

+ **Limited Support Systems:** Many organizations lack support systems, such as employee resource groups (ERGs) or mentorship programs, that can provide LGBTQ employees with the necessary resources and support [?].

## Strategies for Promoting LGBTQ-Friendly Workplaces

To foster LGBTQ-friendly workplaces, organizations can implement several strategies:

+ **Develop Comprehensive Policies:** Organizations should establish clear anti-discrimination policies that specifically include sexual orientation and gender identity. This sends a strong message that discrimination will not be tolerated.

+ **Provide Training and Education:** Regular training sessions on LGBTQ issues for all employees can help raise awareness and foster a culture of respect and inclusion. Training should cover topics such as unconscious bias, microaggressions, and the importance of using correct pronouns [?].

+ **Create Employee Resource Groups (ERGs):** Establishing ERGs for LGBTQ employees can provide a support network, foster community, and offer a platform for advocacy within the organization [?].

+ **Implement Inclusive Benefits:** Offering benefits that cater to the needs of LGBTQ employees, such as same-sex partner benefits and gender-affirming healthcare, is essential for demonstrating commitment to inclusivity [?].

+ **Encourage Open Dialogue:** Organizations should create an environment where employees feel comfortable discussing LGBTQ issues. This can be achieved through open forums, town halls, or anonymous feedback mechanisms [?].

+ **Celebrate LGBTQ Events:** Participating in or sponsoring LGBTQ events, such as Pride Month celebrations, can help demonstrate an organization's commitment to inclusivity and support for the LGBTQ community [?].

## Case Studies

Several organizations have successfully implemented LGBTQ-friendly practices:

+ **Salesforce:** This cloud-based software company has been recognized for its commitment to LGBTQ inclusion. Salesforce provides comprehensive benefits for LGBTQ employees, including gender transition support and has established a strong ERG for LGBTQ employees [?].

+ **Accenture:** Accenture has been a leader in promoting LGBTQ rights within the workplace. The company actively engages in advocacy, provides extensive training on LGBTQ issues, and has received a perfect score on the Human Rights Campaign's Corporate Equality Index for several years [?].

+ **Google:** Google has developed a robust framework for supporting LGBTQ employees, including comprehensive anti-discrimination policies, inclusive benefits, and active participation in LGBTQ advocacy initiatives. Google's Pride Network has fostered a strong sense of community and support among LGBTQ employees [?].

## Conclusion

Promoting LGBTQ-friendly workplaces is not just a moral imperative; it is essential for fostering a productive, innovative, and engaged workforce. By addressing the challenges and implementing effective strategies, organizations can create an environment where all employees, regardless of their sexual orientation or gender identity, can thrive. As the fight for LGBTQ rights continues, workplaces must evolve to become safe havens for diversity and inclusion, paving the way for a more equitable future.

# Combating Workplace Discrimination

Workplace discrimination against LGBTQ individuals remains a pervasive issue in many societies, including Myanmar. This form of discrimination can manifest in various ways, including hiring biases, unequal pay, harassment, and lack of promotion opportunities. Combating workplace discrimination is crucial not only for the well-being of LGBTQ employees but also for fostering inclusive environments that benefit organizations as a whole.

## Understanding Workplace Discrimination

Workplace discrimination can be defined as the unfair treatment of employees based on their sexual orientation, gender identity, or expression. This discrimination can be both overt and subtle, often leading to hostile work environments. According to the *Theory of Organizational Justice*, perceived fairness in the workplace is essential for employee satisfaction and performance. Discrimination undermines this fairness, leading to decreased morale and productivity.

## Theoretical Frameworks

To effectively combat workplace discrimination, several theoretical frameworks can be applied:

- **Social Identity Theory:** This theory posits that individuals derive part of their identity from the social groups to which they belong. Discrimination can negatively impact the self-esteem and mental health of LGBTQ individuals, leading to lower job satisfaction and higher turnover rates.

- **Intersectionality:** This framework emphasizes that individuals experience discrimination differently based on multiple identities, including race, gender, and sexual orientation. Understanding intersectionality is crucial for addressing the unique challenges faced by LGBTQ individuals who belong to other marginalized groups.

+ **Organizational Culture Theory:** This theory highlights the importance of an inclusive organizational culture that promotes diversity. A positive culture can mitigate discrimination and foster a sense of belonging among LGBTQ employees.

## Challenges in Combating Workplace Discrimination

Despite the theoretical frameworks available, several challenges hinder the effective combating of workplace discrimination:

+ **Cultural Norms and Stigma:** In Myanmar, traditional cultural norms often stigmatize LGBTQ identities, leading to widespread discrimination in the workplace. Many organizations may not prioritize diversity and inclusion, viewing LGBTQ issues as secondary.

+ **Lack of Legal Protections:** The absence of comprehensive anti-discrimination laws in Myanmar leaves LGBTQ individuals vulnerable to workplace discrimination without legal recourse. This lack of protection can deter individuals from reporting discrimination or seeking justice.

+ **Fear of Retaliation:** Many LGBTQ employees fear retaliation if they speak out against discrimination. This fear can lead to a culture of silence, where individuals endure mistreatment rather than risk their jobs.

## Strategies for Combating Workplace Discrimination

To combat workplace discrimination effectively, organizations can implement several strategies:

+ **Implementing Inclusive Policies:** Organizations should develop and enforce anti-discrimination policies that explicitly protect LGBTQ employees. These policies should be communicated clearly to all staff and integrated into the organization's culture.

+ **Training and Education:** Providing training on diversity and inclusion can help raise awareness about LGBTQ issues and reduce bias among employees. Workshops that focus on empathy and understanding can foster a more inclusive workplace environment.

+ **Creating Safe Reporting Mechanisms:** Establishing confidential reporting mechanisms allows employees to report discrimination without fear of retaliation. Organizations should ensure that reports are taken seriously and addressed promptly.

+ **Promoting LGBTQ Visibility:** Celebrating LGBTQ events, such as Pride Month, and encouraging employees to share their stories can promote visibility and acceptance within the organization. This visibility can help normalize LGBTQ identities and reduce stigma.

+ **Engaging with LGBTQ Organizations:** Partnering with local LGBTQ organizations can provide organizations with resources and support for creating inclusive workplaces. These partnerships can also help organizations stay informed about best practices in LGBTQ inclusion.

## Examples of Successful Initiatives

Several organizations around the world have successfully implemented initiatives to combat workplace discrimination:

+ **Google:** Google has established comprehensive diversity and inclusion programs, including employee resource groups for LGBTQ employees. The company actively promotes LGBTQ visibility and has been recognized for its inclusive workplace culture.

+ **Salesforce:** Salesforce has implemented policies that prohibit discrimination based on sexual orientation and gender identity. The company provides extensive training on LGBTQ issues and fosters an inclusive environment through various initiatives.

+ **Myanmar Organizations:** Local NGOs in Myanmar have started to advocate for LGBTQ rights in the workplace, collaborating with businesses to promote inclusive practices. These initiatives include training sessions and workshops aimed at reducing discrimination and fostering acceptance.

## Conclusion

Combating workplace discrimination against LGBTQ individuals is essential for creating inclusive and equitable work environments. By understanding the challenges and implementing effective strategies, organizations can foster a culture of acceptance and support. This not only benefits LGBTQ employees but also enhances overall organizational performance and morale. As Myanmar continues to navigate the complexities of LGBTQ rights, the fight against workplace discrimination remains a critical component of the broader movement for equality and justice.

## Building Alliances with LGBTQ-Friendly Businesses

In the journey towards achieving LGBTQ rights and acceptance, building alliances with LGBTQ-friendly businesses plays a crucial role. These partnerships not only provide economic support for the community but also foster a culture of inclusivity and acceptance within the broader society. This section explores the theoretical underpinnings, the challenges faced, and examples of successful collaborations between LGBTQ activists and businesses.

### Theoretical Framework

The concept of Corporate Social Responsibility (CSR) serves as a foundational theory for understanding the role of businesses in supporting social causes, including LGBTQ rights. According to [?], CSR encompasses the economic, legal, ethical, and discretionary expectations that society has of organizations at a given point in time. Businesses that actively engage in LGBTQ advocacy are often viewed as fulfilling their ethical responsibilities, which can enhance their brand image and customer loyalty.

Furthermore, the theory of Intersectionality, as articulated by [?], highlights the interconnected nature of social categorizations such as race, class, and gender. This framework is essential in understanding how LGBTQ individuals navigate their identities within the context of their workplaces. By forming alliances with LGBTQ-friendly businesses, activists can address multiple layers of discrimination and promote a more holistic approach to equality.

### Challenges in Building Alliances

Despite the potential benefits, several challenges hinder the establishment of effective partnerships between LGBTQ activists and businesses:

+ **Tokenism:** Many businesses may engage with LGBTQ issues superficially, using Pride Month as a marketing opportunity without making substantive changes within their organizations. This tokenism can undermine genuine efforts for advocacy and support.

+ **Fear of Backlash:** Businesses may hesitate to align themselves with LGBTQ causes due to fears of alienating conservative customers or facing backlash from anti-LGBTQ groups. This fear can stifle potential partnerships and limit the impact of advocacy efforts.

+ **Lack of Awareness:** Some business leaders may lack knowledge about LGBTQ issues and the importance of inclusivity. This gap in understanding can lead to missed opportunities for collaboration and support.

## Successful Examples of Collaboration

Despite these challenges, there have been several successful examples of alliances between LGBTQ activists and businesses that demonstrate the potential for positive impact:

+ **The Human Rights Campaign (HRC) Corporate Equality Index:** This initiative rates businesses on their LGBTQ-inclusive policies and practices. Companies that score well not only improve their public image but also attract LGBTQ talent and customers. For instance, tech giants like Google and Apple have consistently ranked high, showcasing their commitment to LGBTQ rights through various programs and policies.

+ **Partnership with Local LGBTQ Organizations:** In Myanmar, businesses such as restaurants and cafes have collaborated with local LGBTQ groups to host events that raise awareness about LGBTQ issues. These events not only provide a platform for activism but also create safe spaces for community members. For example, a local café in Yangon hosted a Pride-themed event, providing visibility and support for LGBTQ artists and activists.

+ **Sponsorship of LGBTQ Events:** Businesses can play a pivotal role in sponsoring LGBTQ events, such as pride parades and awareness campaigns. This sponsorship not only provides financial support but also signals to the community that the business is an ally. For instance, a local fashion brand in Myanmar sponsored a pride march, showcasing its commitment to diversity and inclusion.

## Strategies for Effective Partnerships

To build effective alliances with LGBTQ-friendly businesses, activists can employ several strategies:

+ **Education and Training:** Conducting workshops and training sessions for business leaders on LGBTQ issues can foster understanding and commitment. These sessions can address the importance of inclusivity and the benefits of supporting LGBTQ rights.

+ **Creating Visibility:** Activists can work with businesses to create visibility around LGBTQ issues through marketing campaigns, social media, and community events. This visibility can help normalize LGBTQ presence in the business sector and encourage other businesses to follow suit.

+ **Developing Long-Term Partnerships:** Establishing long-term relationships with businesses rather than one-off collaborations can lead to sustained support for LGBTQ initiatives. This can be achieved through regular communication, shared goals, and mutual accountability.

## Conclusion

Building alliances with LGBTQ-friendly businesses is a vital component of the broader LGBTQ rights movement in Myanmar. Through strategic partnerships, activists can amplify their voices, create safe spaces, and foster a culture of acceptance within the business community. By overcoming challenges and leveraging successful examples, the LGBTQ community can continue to make strides towards equality and inclusion.

# The Global Impact of LGBTQ Activism in Myanmar

## The Global Impact of LGBTQ Activism in Myanmar

### The Global Impact of LGBTQ Activism in Myanmar

The global impact of LGBTQ activism in Myanmar is a testament to the interconnectedness of social movements across borders. As LGBTQ activists in Myanmar navigate the complexities of their cultural and political landscape, their efforts resonate far beyond their national context, influencing international discourse on human rights and social justice. This section explores the multifaceted ways in which LGBTQ activism in Myanmar has garnered global attention and sparked solidarity movements worldwide.

At the heart of this activism lies the recognition of LGBTQ rights as human rights. The Universal Declaration of Human Rights (UDHR) asserts that "All human beings are born free and equal in dignity and rights." This foundational principle has been a rallying cry for activists in Myanmar, who face systemic discrimination and violence. The struggle for LGBTQ rights in Myanmar challenges not only local norms but also engages with international human rights frameworks.

One significant aspect of the global impact of Myanmar's LGBTQ activism is the sharing of personal narratives. Activists have utilized social media platforms to tell their stories, breaking the silence surrounding LGBTQ experiences in a conservative society. For example, the hashtag #MyanmarPride gained traction on platforms like Twitter and Instagram, allowing individuals to share their journeys of self-acceptance and resilience. This digital storytelling has not only fostered a sense of community within Myanmar but has also attracted international attention, drawing support from global human rights organizations.

Moreover, the participation of Myanmar activists in international LGBTQ conferences has been pivotal in amplifying their voices. Events such as the International Lesbian, Gay, Bisexual, Trans and Intersex Association (ILGA) World Conference provide a platform for activists to network, share strategies, and collaborate with allies from around the world. For instance, during the 2019 ILGA conference in Taipei, activists from Myanmar presented their challenges and successes, garnering solidarity and support from international attendees. This engagement has led to increased visibility for Myanmar's LGBTQ issues and has inspired activism in other regions facing similar challenges.

The influence of Myanmar's LGBTQ activism extends to international human rights policies. Activists have actively engaged with bodies like the United Nations to advocate for LGBTQ-inclusive international agreements. The 2016 UN Free & Equal campaign, which promotes equal rights for LGBTQ individuals globally, has seen participation from Myanmar activists who highlight the unique struggles faced by LGBTQ communities in Southeast Asia. By confronting LGBTQ rights violations at the UN, they have contributed to a broader discourse on the necessity of recognizing sexual orientation and gender identity in human rights frameworks.

Additionally, the collaboration with global LGBTQ allies has strengthened the movement in Myanmar. Organizations such as Human Rights Watch and Amnesty International have provided crucial support, conducting research and publishing reports on the human rights situation for LGBTQ individuals in Myanmar. These reports have not only raised awareness but have also pressured the Myanmar government to reconsider its stance on LGBTQ rights. The global spotlight created by these collaborations has made it increasingly difficult for local authorities to ignore the calls for change.

The ripple effect of LGBTQ activism in Myanmar is also evident in its intersectionality with other social justice movements. Activists have recognized the importance of engaging in women's rights advocacy and fighting for ethnic minority rights. This intersectional approach has enriched the activism landscape, fostering solidarity among diverse groups facing oppression. For example, during the 2020 protests against the military coup in Myanmar, LGBTQ activists joined forces with women's rights organizations, emphasizing the need for an inclusive movement that addresses the needs of all marginalized communities.

However, the journey is fraught with challenges. The activists often face backlash not only from the state but also from conservative segments of society. The criminalization of homosexuality in Myanmar remains a significant barrier, creating an environment where LGBTQ individuals are vulnerable to violence and discrimination. Despite these challenges, activists continue to push for change, drawing strength from their global allies and the solidarity they have cultivated.

In conclusion, the global impact of LGBTQ activism in Myanmar is a powerful illustration of how local struggles can resonate on an international scale. Through storytelling, participation in global forums, and collaboration with international allies, Myanmar's LGBTQ activists have not only raised awareness of their plight but have also contributed to the broader movement for human rights. Their resilience and commitment to social justice serve as an inspiration to activists worldwide, highlighting the importance of solidarity in the fight for equality. The journey is ongoing, but the seeds of change have been sown, promising a more inclusive future for LGBTQ individuals in Myanmar and beyond.

# Sharing Myanmar's LGBTQ Story

## Engaging with International Media

Engaging with international media is a critical component of LGBTQ activism, particularly in a country like Myanmar, where local narratives may be overshadowed by traditional values and governmental censorship. The ability to convey personal stories and the broader struggles of the LGBTQ community to a global audience can significantly impact public perception and policy change.

## The Power of Storytelling

At the heart of effective media engagement lies the art of storytelling. Activists like Wai Wai Nu have harnessed the power of personal narratives to humanize the LGBTQ experience in Myanmar. As the renowned activist Audre Lorde once said, "Your silence will not protect you." This sentiment underscores the importance of visibility. By sharing their stories, activists can challenge stereotypes and foster empathy among audiences who may be unfamiliar with the complexities of LGBTQ identities.

$$\text{Visibility} = \frac{\text{Personal Narratives}}{\text{Cultural Stigmas}} \qquad (26)$$

This equation illustrates that increased visibility can be achieved by amplifying personal narratives in proportion to the cultural stigmas that often silence them. By engaging with international media, activists can ensure that their stories reach a wider audience, thus fostering a more inclusive dialogue.

## Strategies for Media Engagement

To effectively engage with international media, LGBTQ activists in Myanmar have employed various strategies:

1. **Press Releases and Media Kits**: Crafting comprehensive press releases that outline key issues, personal stories, and calls to action can attract media attention. Media kits should include background information on the LGBTQ movement in Myanmar, statistics on discrimination, and profiles of local activists.

2. **Social Media Utilization**: Platforms like Twitter, Instagram, and Facebook have become essential tools for activists. By sharing updates, personal stories, and engaging visuals, activists can create a narrative that resonates with both local and international audiences.

3. **Collaborations with Journalists**: Building relationships with sympathetic journalists can lead to in-depth features and interviews that highlight the LGBTQ plight in Myanmar. Activists can provide journalists with insights and context that elevate their reporting.

4. **Participating in Documentaries and Interviews**: Engaging in visual storytelling through documentaries or interviews can powerfully convey the LGBTQ experience. Documentaries can serve as a potent medium to reach audiences who may not otherwise engage with LGBTQ issues.

5. **Leveraging International Events**: Activists can take advantage of international events such as Pride Month or Human Rights Day to amplify their message. By participating in global discussions and sharing their experiences, they can draw attention to the unique challenges faced by LGBTQ individuals in Myanmar.

## Challenges in Media Engagement

Despite the potential benefits, engaging with international media also presents challenges:

- **Censorship and Misinformation**: Activists must navigate a landscape where misinformation is rampant and censorship is common. Ensuring accurate representation of LGBTQ issues is paramount, yet difficult in a context where media narratives are often controlled by government interests.

- **Cultural Sensitivity**: International media may not always grasp the nuances of local culture. Activists must work to educate journalists about the sociopolitical context of Myanmar, ensuring that coverage does not perpetuate stereotypes or misunderstandings.

- **Safety Concerns**: Activists face real risks when engaging with media. Exposure can lead to harassment or violence, particularly in conservative environments. Therefore, it is crucial for activists to prioritize their safety and the safety of their communities when sharing their stories.

## Examples of Successful Media Engagement

Several instances of successful media engagement highlight the effectiveness of these strategies:

- **Wai Wai Nu's Advocacy**: By participating in international panels and media interviews, Wai Wai Nu has successfully brought attention to the plight of LGBTQ individuals in Myanmar. Her story has been featured in major publications, helping to shift perceptions and garner international support.
- **Documentary Features**: Documentaries such as "My Myanmar" have showcased the vibrant yet challenging lives of LGBTQ individuals in Myanmar, providing a platform for their voices to be heard on a global scale.
- **Social Media Campaigns**: The use of hashtags like #LGBTQMyanmar has allowed activists to connect with a global audience, fostering solidarity and support from international allies.

In conclusion, engaging with international media is an essential avenue for LGBTQ activists in Myanmar to share their stories, challenge discrimination, and advocate for change. By employing effective strategies while navigating the inherent challenges, activists can amplify their voices and foster a more inclusive global dialogue about LGBTQ rights. The journey is fraught with obstacles, but the potential for impact is immense, as the world becomes increasingly interconnected and aware of the diverse struggles for human rights.

# Participating in International LGBTQ Conferences

Participating in international LGBTQ conferences has been a pivotal aspect of Wai Wai Nu's activism, providing a platform for sharing experiences, strategies, and building global solidarity. These conferences serve as a critical space for activists from diverse backgrounds to converge, exchange ideas, and amplify their voices in the fight for equality and rights.

## The Importance of Global Networking

One of the primary benefits of attending international LGBTQ conferences is the opportunity for networking. Activists like Wai Wai Nu can connect with peers from different countries, each bringing unique perspectives and approaches to activism.

This networking fosters collaboration and the sharing of resources, which can be instrumental in strengthening local movements.

For instance, during the International LGBTQ Pride Conference in 2018, Wai Wai Nu met activists from various regions who were facing similar challenges in their fight against discrimination. This encounter led to the establishment of a coalition that worked on joint campaigns to raise awareness about the plight of LGBTQ individuals in regions where rights are severely restricted. The collective effort resulted in a significant increase in media coverage and international attention on the issue.

## Advocating for Policy Changes

Conferences also provide a platform for advocating for policy changes at an international level. Activists can engage with policymakers, human rights organizations, and influential figures in the LGBTQ movement. This engagement is crucial for pushing for inclusive policies and legal reforms in their respective countries.

Wai Wai Nu's participation in the 2019 Global LGBTQ Rights Summit allowed her to present a case study on the legal challenges faced by LGBTQ individuals in Myanmar. Her presentation highlighted the criminalization of homosexuality under Section 377 of the Penal Code, which has been a significant barrier to achieving equality. By sharing her insights, she not only raised awareness about the specific challenges in Myanmar but also garnered support from international allies who could advocate for change on her behalf.

## Educational Workshops and Capacity Building

International conferences often include workshops and training sessions designed to equip activists with the necessary skills and knowledge to enhance their advocacy efforts. These educational components cover a range of topics, including legal rights, mental health support, and community organizing strategies.

For example, at the 2020 International LGBTQ Activism Workshop, Wai Wai Nu participated in a session focused on digital activism. The workshop provided insights into utilizing social media effectively to mobilize support and raise awareness about LGBTQ issues. This training proved invaluable as she later implemented these strategies in Myanmar, leading to a successful online campaign that highlighted the stories of LGBTQ individuals facing discrimination.

## Building Solidarity and Awareness

The act of participating in these conferences also serves to build solidarity among LGBTQ activists globally. By sharing personal narratives and the struggles faced in their home countries, activists like Wai Wai Nu contribute to a broader understanding of the intersectionality of LGBTQ rights.

The stories shared at these conferences resonate deeply, fostering empathy and support among attendees. For instance, during a panel discussion at the 2021 World LGBTQ Rights Forum, Wai Wai Nu recounted her journey of activism amidst the backdrop of Myanmar's political landscape. Her emotional appeal not only moved her audience but also inspired many to take action in their own communities.

## Challenges Faced at Conferences

Despite the numerous benefits, participating in international LGBTQ conferences is not without its challenges. Activists from countries with oppressive regimes often face difficulties in obtaining visas, risking their safety, or dealing with backlash upon their return home.

Wai Wai Nu encountered such challenges when attempting to attend the 2022 International LGBTQ Rights Conference in Europe. The Myanmar government had recently intensified its crackdown on dissent, leading to heightened scrutiny of activists traveling abroad. To mitigate risks, she had to navigate complex visa processes and ensure her safety while abroad, underscoring the precarious nature of activism in repressive environments.

## Theoretical Framework: Intersectionality in Activism

The concept of intersectionality is crucial in understanding the dynamics of international LGBTQ conferences. Coined by Kimberlé Crenshaw, intersectionality refers to the ways in which various forms of discrimination overlap and intersect, impacting individuals' experiences differently based on their identities.

In the context of LGBTQ activism, this theory highlights the importance of recognizing how factors such as race, gender, and socioeconomic status influence the challenges faced by activists. For instance, Wai Wai Nu's identity as a Rohingya woman adds layers of complexity to her activism, as she navigates both LGBTQ issues and ethnic discrimination.

## Conclusion

In conclusion, participating in international LGBTQ conferences has been instrumental for Wai Wai Nu in her quest for equality and justice for LGBTQ individuals in Myanmar. These gatherings offer invaluable opportunities for networking, advocacy, education, and solidarity-building. While challenges persist, the collective strength and shared experiences gained from these conferences continue to empower activists like Wai Wai Nu to push forward in their fight for a more inclusive and equitable world.

$$\text{Advocacy Success} = f(\text{Networking, Education, Solidarity}) \qquad (27)$$

# Collaborating with Global LGBTQ Allies

In the pursuit of LGBTQ rights in Myanmar, collaboration with global allies has proven to be a pivotal strategy in amplifying voices, sharing resources, and fostering solidarity across borders. This section examines the theoretical underpinnings of such collaborations, the challenges faced, and the successful examples that have emerged from these partnerships.

## Theoretical Framework

The collaboration between local activists and global allies can be understood through the lens of *transnational advocacy networks* (TANs). According to Keck and Sikkink (1998), TANs are defined as "a set of relevant actors working internationally on an issue, bound together by shared values, a common discourse, and dense exchanges of information and services." These networks enable local activists to leverage international attention and resources, thereby enhancing their capacity to effect change.

In the context of Myanmar, the intersectionality of LGBTQ rights with broader human rights issues necessitates a multi-faceted approach to advocacy. This aligns with Crenshaw's (1989) theory of intersectionality, which posits that individuals experience oppression in varying configurations and degrees of intensity based on their overlapping identities. Collaborating with global allies allows for a more nuanced understanding of how local LGBTQ issues intersect with global human rights frameworks.

## Challenges in Collaboration

Despite the potential benefits, collaborating with global LGBTQ allies is fraught with challenges. One significant issue is the *cultural disconnect* that can arise when international organizations impose their frameworks and strategies without fully understanding the local context. For instance, a campaign that works effectively in Western nations may not resonate with the cultural and social dynamics present in Myanmar. This can lead to a sense of alienation among local activists, who may feel that their voices are being overshadowed by more dominant narratives.

Additionally, there is the challenge of *resource dependency*. Local activists often rely on funding and support from international NGOs, which can create a power imbalance. This dependency can lead to situations where the priorities of global allies overshadow local needs, resulting in initiatives that do not align with the community's actual concerns.

## Successful Examples of Collaboration

Despite these challenges, there are notable successes that highlight the effectiveness of global collaboration. One such example is the partnership between Myanmar's LGBTQ activists and organizations like *OutRight Action International* and *ILGA World*. These organizations have provided critical support in terms of capacity building, funding, and international advocacy.

A key initiative was the *Myanmar LGBTQ Rights Forum*, which brought together activists from Myanmar and representatives from international organizations to discuss strategies for advancing LGBTQ rights. This forum not only facilitated knowledge exchange but also helped to build a unified front in advocating for legal reforms in Myanmar.

Moreover, during the United Nations Human Rights Council sessions, Myanmar LGBTQ activists collaborated with global allies to present reports on human rights violations faced by LGBTQ individuals in Myanmar. This collaboration resulted in increased international pressure on the Myanmar government to address these issues, demonstrating the power of unified advocacy efforts.

## Building Solidarity with Global Movements

Collaborating with global LGBTQ allies also opens avenues for building solidarity with movements in other countries facing similar challenges. For instance, Myanmar activists have drawn parallels with the struggles of LGBTQ individuals in countries like Uganda and Russia, where anti-LGBTQ laws are prevalent. By sharing experiences and strategies, activists can foster a sense of global camaraderie that transcends national boundaries.

This solidarity is crucial for sustaining momentum in the fight for LGBTQ rights. When activists from different regions come together, they can amplify each other's messages, share resources, and create a more robust global network of support.

## Conclusion

In conclusion, collaborating with global LGBTQ allies is an essential component of advancing LGBTQ rights in Myanmar. While challenges such as cultural disconnect and resource dependency persist, the benefits of shared knowledge, solidarity, and international advocacy far outweigh these obstacles. By engaging with global networks, Myanmar activists can enhance their visibility, access vital resources, and ultimately work towards a more equitable society for all LGBTQ individuals. The journey towards equality is undoubtedly complex, but through collaboration, the path becomes clearer and more attainable.

## Networking with LGBTQ Activists Worldwide

In the global landscape of LGBTQ activism, networking plays a pivotal role in fostering solidarity, sharing resources, and amplifying voices that often go unheard. For activists like Wai Wai Nu, building connections with LGBTQ advocates worldwide has not only enriched their understanding of global issues but has also provided a platform for collaborative action. This section delves into the significance of networking within the LGBTQ community, the challenges faced, and the tangible outcomes of these international alliances.

### The Importance of Global Connections

Networking with LGBTQ activists worldwide allows for the exchange of ideas, strategies, and experiences that can enhance local movements. As theorized by social network theory, the strength of weak ties can provide access to new information and resources that are not available within one's immediate circle [?]. This is particularly relevant in the context of LGBTQ activism, where local activists may face isolation due to societal stigmas or legal restrictions.

For instance, Wai Wai Nu's involvement in international conferences, such as the International Lesbian, Gay, Bisexual, Trans and Intersex Association (ILGA) meetings, has facilitated connections with activists from various cultural backgrounds. These interactions have led to the sharing of best practices in advocacy, which have been adapted to fit the unique context of Myanmar.

## Challenges in Networking

Despite the potential benefits, networking is not without its challenges. Activists often confront barriers such as language differences, cultural misunderstandings, and varying levels of access to technology. In many regions, including Myanmar, internet censorship can hinder communication and limit the ability to engage with global networks.

Moreover, the intersectionality of identities within the LGBTQ community can complicate networking efforts. Activists must navigate not only sexual orientation and gender identity but also ethnic, economic, and geographic differences. These complexities can lead to misunderstandings or the marginalization of certain groups within the broader movement [?].

## Examples of Successful Networking

One notable example of successful networking is the collaboration between Myanmar's LGBTQ activists and international organizations such as OutRight Action International. Through joint campaigns and advocacy efforts, these partnerships have raised awareness about the legal and social challenges faced by LGBTQ individuals in Myanmar. The collaboration has resulted in increased funding for local initiatives, enabling activists to organize community events and awareness campaigns that highlight the importance of LGBTQ rights.

Additionally, social media platforms have emerged as vital tools for networking. Activists utilize platforms like Twitter, Instagram, and Facebook to share their stories, mobilize support, and connect with allies globally. The hashtag campaigns, such as #LoveIsLove and #LGBTQMyanmar, have not only garnered international attention but have also created a sense of community among activists facing similar struggles.

## The Role of International Conferences

International conferences serve as crucial spaces for networking among LGBTQ activists. Events like the World Pride and the Global Forum on MSM and HIV (MSMGF) provide opportunities for activists to share their experiences, learn from one another, and strategize on collective actions. These gatherings often feature workshops, panel discussions, and networking sessions that foster collaboration across borders.

For example, during the 2019 ILGA World Conference held in Wellington, New Zealand, activists from Myanmar were able to present their work and challenges, receiving feedback and support from global leaders in the LGBTQ movement. Such interactions not only validate the struggles faced by local activists but also inspire innovative approaches to advocacy.

## Conclusion

In conclusion, networking with LGBTQ activists worldwide is a vital component of building a robust and resilient movement for LGBTQ rights. While challenges exist, the benefits of shared knowledge, resources, and solidarity far outweigh the obstacles. As Wai Wai Nu continues to forge connections with global allies, the potential for impactful change within Myanmar and beyond remains promising. The ongoing exchange of ideas and strategies will undoubtedly strengthen the resolve of activists and contribute to a more inclusive and equitable world for LGBTQ individuals.

## Building Solidarity with LGBTQ Movements in Other Countries

Building solidarity with LGBTQ movements in other countries is an essential strategy for amplifying the voices of marginalized communities and fostering a global network of support. This section explores the theoretical frameworks, challenges, and practical examples of how LGBTQ activists in Myanmar can and have engaged with their counterparts internationally.

### Theoretical Frameworks

Solidarity in social movements is often grounded in the principles of intersectionality and transnationalism. Intersectionality, coined by Kimberlé Crenshaw, emphasizes the interconnectedness of various social identities and the unique experiences of individuals who navigate multiple forms of discrimination. For LGBTQ individuals in Myanmar, this means recognizing that their struggles are intertwined with issues of ethnicity, class, and gender. Transnationalism, on the other hand, refers to the flow of ideas, resources, and support across national boundaries, allowing for a collective movement that transcends local limitations.

These frameworks provide a foundation for understanding how local LGBTQ movements can connect with global struggles for equality. By acknowledging the shared experiences of oppression and the diverse contexts in which they occur, activists can create a more unified front against discrimination.

## Challenges in Building Solidarity

Despite the theoretical benefits of solidarity, several challenges hinder the effective collaboration between LGBTQ movements in Myanmar and those in other countries:

+ **Cultural Differences:** Different cultural contexts can lead to misunderstandings and misinterpretations of LGBTQ identities and issues. Activists must navigate these differences sensitively to avoid imposing Western ideals onto local struggles.

+ **Resource Disparities:** Many LGBTQ organizations in Myanmar operate with limited resources compared to their counterparts in more developed countries. This disparity can create power imbalances in partnerships, where the voices of local activists may be overshadowed by those from wealthier nations.

+ **Political Repression:** Activists in Myanmar face significant risks, including harassment and imprisonment. This environment can make it difficult to engage openly with international allies, as the fear of surveillance and retaliation looms large.

+ **Fragmentation of Movements:** The LGBTQ community is not monolithic; it encompasses a wide range of identities and experiences. Fragmentation within movements can complicate solidarity efforts, as differing priorities and goals may lead to conflicts or competition for resources.

## Examples of Solidarity in Action

Despite these challenges, there are numerous examples of successful solidarity-building efforts between LGBTQ movements in Myanmar and those around the world:

+ **International Conferences:** Participation in international LGBTQ conferences, such as the International Lesbian, Gay, Bisexual, Trans and Intersex Association (ILGA) World Conference, allows activists from Myanmar to share their experiences and learn from others. These platforms foster networking opportunities and facilitate the exchange of strategies for advocacy.

+ **Social Media Campaigns:** Social media has become a powerful tool for building solidarity across borders. Campaigns like #PrideAcrossBorders enable LGBTQ activists to share their stories and challenges, creating a sense of global community. For instance, Myanmar activists have used platforms like Twitter and Facebook to raise awareness about their struggles, drawing international attention and support.

+ **Collaborative Projects:** Partnerships with international NGOs have led to collaborative projects aimed at capacity building. For example, training workshops led by global LGBTQ organizations have equipped Myanmar activists with essential skills in advocacy, media engagement, and legal reform.

+ **Global Fundraising Initiatives:** Fundraising efforts that span multiple countries can provide much-needed resources for local movements. Initiatives like the Global Fund for Women have supported LGBTQ projects in Myanmar, helping to sustain activism in the face of political and economic challenges.

## Conclusion

Building solidarity with LGBTQ movements in other countries is not only a strategic necessity but also a moral imperative. By forging connections, sharing resources, and amplifying each other's voices, activists can create a more robust and resilient global movement for LGBTQ rights. As Wai Wai Nu and her peers continue to advocate for change in Myanmar, their efforts will be strengthened by the solidarity and support of international allies who recognize the importance of unity in the fight for equality.

In summary, the journey towards building solidarity is fraught with challenges, yet the potential for transformative change remains high. By embracing intersectionality and transnationalism, LGBTQ activists in Myanmar can navigate these complexities and contribute to a global narrative that champions diversity, resilience, and justice for all.

# Influencing International Human Rights Policies

## Advocating for LGBTQ-Inclusive International Agreements

The advocacy for LGBTQ-inclusive international agreements has emerged as a critical aspect of the global human rights discourse. As societies grapple with the complexities of gender and sexual diversity, the need for comprehensive legal frameworks that protect LGBTQ individuals becomes increasingly urgent. This section delves into the theoretical foundations, existing challenges, and practical examples of advocating for such agreements.

## Theoretical Foundations

The advocacy for LGBTQ-inclusive international agreements is rooted in several key theoretical frameworks:

+ **Human Rights Theory:** At its core, the fight for LGBTQ rights is a struggle for basic human rights. The Universal Declaration of Human Rights (UDHR), adopted by the United Nations in 1948, asserts that "all human beings are born free and equal in dignity and rights." This principle serves as a foundation for advocating against discrimination based on sexual orientation and gender identity.

+ **Intersectionality:** Coined by Kimberlé Crenshaw, intersectionality is vital in understanding how various forms of discrimination overlap. LGBTQ individuals often face compounded discrimination based on race, ethnicity, socioeconomic status, and other identities. Advocating for inclusive agreements necessitates a nuanced understanding of these intersections to ensure that all voices are heard.

+ **Social Justice Theory:** This theory emphasizes the need for equitable distribution of resources and opportunities. LGBTQ-inclusive agreements can be seen as a means to address systemic inequalities and promote social justice on a global scale.

## Challenges in Advocacy

Despite the theoretical underpinnings, several challenges hinder the advancement of LGBTQ-inclusive international agreements:

+ **Cultural Resistance:** In many countries, cultural norms and religious beliefs perpetuate homophobia and transphobia. This resistance can create significant barriers to the adoption of inclusive agreements, as governments may prioritize traditional values over universal human rights.

+ **Political Will:** The lack of political will among certain states can stall the progress of LGBTQ rights. Governments may fear backlash from conservative constituents, leading to a reluctance to engage in discussions about LGBTQ inclusion in international agreements.

+ **Legal Frameworks:** Existing legal frameworks in many nations criminalize homosexuality or do not recognize gender identity. This creates a discord between national laws and international human rights obligations, complicating advocacy efforts.

## Practical Examples

Several initiatives and agreements illustrate the advocacy for LGBTQ-inclusive international agreements:

+ **The Yogyakarta Principles:** Developed in 2006, the Yogyakarta Principles provide a framework for applying international human rights law to issues of sexual orientation and gender identity. They serve as a guide for states to create inclusive policies and laws, promoting accountability and adherence to human rights obligations.

+ **UN Free & Equal Campaign:** Launched by the United Nations Human Rights Office, this campaign aims to raise awareness about LGBTQ rights and promote equality worldwide. Through advocacy, education, and outreach, the campaign seeks to influence international agreements and national policies to protect LGBTQ individuals.

+ **The 2016 UN Resolution on Human Rights, Sexual Orientation, and Gender Identity:** This groundbreaking resolution marked a significant step toward recognizing LGBTQ rights within the UN framework. It calls for an end to violence and discrimination based on sexual orientation and gender identity, urging member states to uphold their human rights obligations.

## Strategies for Effective Advocacy

To effectively advocate for LGBTQ-inclusive international agreements, several strategies can be employed:

+ **Building Coalitions:** Collaboration among LGBTQ organizations, human rights groups, and allies is essential. By pooling resources and expertise, advocates can amplify their voices and increase their influence on international platforms.

+ **Engaging with International Bodies:** Actively participating in UN meetings, conferences, and forums allows advocates to present their cases and push for the inclusion of LGBTQ rights in international agreements. Engaging with diplomats and policymakers is crucial for fostering understanding and support.

+ **Utilizing Media and Technology:** Social media and traditional media play a vital role in raising awareness and mobilizing support. Advocates can leverage these platforms to share stories, highlight injustices, and rally global support for LGBTQ-inclusive agreements.

## Conclusion

Advocating for LGBTQ-inclusive international agreements is a multifaceted endeavor that requires a deep understanding of human rights theory, recognition of the challenges faced, and the implementation of effective strategies. As the global landscape continues to evolve, the commitment to inclusivity and equality must remain steadfast. By fostering collaboration, engaging with international bodies, and utilizing media, advocates can pave the way for a future where LGBTQ rights are universally recognized and protected.

In the words of Wai Wai Nu, "We must continue to fight, not just for ourselves, but for the generations to come. The struggle for LGBTQ rights is a struggle for human rights, and it is a fight that we will win together."

# Confronting LGBTQ Rights Violations at the United Nations

The United Nations (UN) serves as a pivotal platform for addressing global human rights issues, including the rights of LGBTQ individuals. Within this framework, confronting LGBTQ rights violations at the UN involves a multifaceted approach that encompasses advocacy, reporting, and collaboration with member states and civil society organizations. This section explores the theoretical underpinnings, the challenges faced, and the significant examples of LGBTQ rights advocacy at the UN.

## Theoretical Framework

The foundation for confronting LGBTQ rights violations at the UN is rooted in international human rights law, which asserts that all individuals, regardless of their sexual orientation or gender identity, are entitled to the same rights and protections. Key documents, such as the Universal Declaration of Human Rights

(UDHR) and the International Covenant on Civil and Political Rights (ICCPR), establish the principle of non-discrimination.

The application of intersectionality theory is also crucial in understanding how various forms of discrimination—based on race, ethnicity, gender, and sexual orientation—intersect to create unique challenges for LGBTQ individuals. This theoretical framework aids advocates in highlighting the compounded nature of rights violations faced by marginalized groups within the LGBTQ community.

## Challenges in Advocacy

Despite the theoretical support for LGBTQ rights, significant challenges persist in effectively confronting violations at the UN. These challenges include:

+ **Political Resistance:** Many member states are resistant to recognizing LGBTQ rights, often citing cultural or religious beliefs as justification for discrimination. This resistance can lead to a lack of political will to address LGBTQ issues at the UN level.

+ **Limited Representation:** LGBTQ individuals and organizations often struggle to gain representation within UN discussions and decision-making processes. This lack of visibility can hinder the ability to advocate for necessary changes.

+ **Safety Concerns:** Activists advocating for LGBTQ rights in oppressive regimes face threats to their safety and freedom. This fear can deter individuals from speaking out or engaging with UN mechanisms.

+ **Fragmented Support:** The LGBTQ rights movement is diverse, encompassing various identities and issues. This fragmentation can lead to competing priorities and dilute the effectiveness of advocacy efforts at the UN.

## Examples of Advocacy Efforts

Several significant examples illustrate the efforts to confront LGBTQ rights violations at the UN:

+ **The Yogyakarta Principles:** Adopted in 2006, these principles articulate international human rights standards in relation to sexual orientation and gender identity. They provide a framework for advocates to hold states accountable for violations. The principles have been referenced in UN discussions and reports, reinforcing the call for LGBTQ rights.

+ **UN Free & Equal Campaign:** Launched by the UN Human Rights Office, this campaign aims to promote equal rights and fair treatment of LGBTQ individuals globally. Through advocacy, education, and outreach, the campaign seeks to combat discrimination and raise awareness of LGBTQ issues within the UN system and beyond.

+ **Reports from Special Rapporteurs:** UN Special Rapporteurs on human rights have published reports highlighting violations against LGBTQ individuals. These reports serve as critical tools for advocacy, providing documentation and recommendations for member states to address discrimination and violence.

+ **The UN Human Rights Council:** The Council has held discussions and adopted resolutions specifically addressing the rights of LGBTQ individuals. For instance, the resolution on "Human Rights, Sexual Orientation and Gender Identity" calls for an end to violence and discrimination based on sexual orientation and gender identity, urging states to protect LGBTQ individuals.

## Engaging with Member States

Effective advocacy at the UN requires collaboration with member states. Engaging with progressive nations that support LGBTQ rights can help amplify the message and apply pressure on those that resist change. This engagement can take various forms:

+ **Bilateral Dialogues:** Advocates can work with supportive governments to address LGBTQ rights violations in countries with poor records. These dialogues can lead to public statements, diplomatic pressure, and targeted assistance for LGBTQ advocacy.

+ **Coalitions and Alliances:** Building coalitions with other human rights organizations and civil society groups can enhance the impact of advocacy efforts. By presenting a united front, activists can draw attention to issues and push for accountability.

+ **Utilizing UN Mechanisms:** Advocates should leverage existing UN mechanisms, such as the Universal Periodic Review (UPR), to highlight

LGBTQ rights violations. The UPR process allows for the examination of human rights records of all UN member states and provides an opportunity for advocates to submit reports and recommendations.

## Conclusion

Confronting LGBTQ rights violations at the United Nations is an ongoing struggle that requires persistence, collaboration, and strategic advocacy. While challenges remain, the efforts of activists and allies continue to push for recognition and protection of LGBTQ rights on the global stage. By leveraging the theoretical frameworks, engaging with member states, and utilizing UN mechanisms, advocates can work towards a future where LGBTQ individuals are afforded the same rights and dignities as all people, regardless of their sexual orientation or gender identity. The journey is fraught with obstacles, but the commitment to justice and equality remains unwavering.

## Promoting LGBTQ Rights in Diplomatic Relations

The promotion of LGBTQ rights in diplomatic relations is a crucial aspect of international human rights advocacy. It involves the integration of LGBTQ issues into the broader framework of foreign policy, ensuring that the rights and dignity of LGBTQ individuals are recognized and protected on a global scale. This section explores the theoretical underpinnings, challenges, and practical examples of how LGBTQ rights can be advanced through diplomatic channels.

### Theoretical Framework

At the core of promoting LGBTQ rights in diplomatic relations lies the theory of **constructivism**, which posits that international relations are shaped by social constructs, including norms, identities, and values. Constructivists argue that states are not just rational actors but are influenced by the ideas and beliefs that prevail in their societies. Thus, the promotion of LGBTQ rights can be seen as a way to reshape international norms and foster a more inclusive global community.

Moreover, the **human rights-based approach** emphasizes that LGBTQ rights are fundamental human rights. This perspective asserts that all individuals, regardless of their sexual orientation or gender identity, deserve protection and equality under the law. Diplomatic efforts that prioritize human rights can leverage international treaties and conventions, such as the *Universal Declaration of Human Rights* (UDHR) and the *International Covenant on Civil and Political Rights* (ICCPR), to advocate for LGBTQ rights.

## Challenges in Promoting LGBTQ Rights

Despite the theoretical support for LGBTQ rights in diplomacy, several challenges persist:

1. **Cultural Relativism**: Many countries justify their discriminatory practices against LGBTQ individuals by invoking cultural or religious beliefs. This often leads to resistance against international pressure to change laws or policies. For instance, some African and Middle Eastern countries have enacted harsh anti-LGBTQ laws, arguing that such measures are consistent with their cultural values.

2. **Political Resistance**: Governments may view the promotion of LGBTQ rights as an infringement on their sovereignty. This resistance can manifest in diplomatic negotiations where LGBTQ rights are sidelined in favor of economic or strategic interests. An example of this is the reluctance of some Western nations to confront human rights abuses in countries with which they have significant trade relationships.

3. **Lack of Political Will**: In many countries, political leaders may lack the will to promote LGBTQ rights due to fear of backlash from conservative constituents. This is evident in countries like Russia, where the government has enacted laws that suppress LGBTQ activism, citing the need to protect traditional family values.

## Examples of Diplomatic Efforts

Despite these challenges, there are notable examples of successful diplomatic efforts to promote LGBTQ rights:

1. **U.S. Foreign Policy**: Under the Obama administration, the U.S. made significant strides in promoting LGBTQ rights globally. The State Department established the **Global Equality Fund**, which supports initiatives aimed at advancing LGBTQ rights in various countries. This fund has been instrumental in providing resources for local activists and organizations working to combat discrimination.

2. **European Union Initiatives**: The European Union has integrated LGBTQ rights into its external relations, conditioning trade agreements on human rights standards. For example, the EU has used its influence to push for LGBTQ rights in negotiations with countries like Uganda, where anti-LGBTQ laws have been a point of contention.

3. **United Nations Advocacy**: The UN has played a pivotal role in promoting LGBTQ rights on the international stage. The establishment of the

UN **Free & Equal** campaign aims to raise awareness and promote equality for LGBTQ individuals worldwide. This initiative has facilitated dialogues between member states, encouraging them to adopt more inclusive policies.

## Strategies for Effective Promotion

To effectively promote LGBTQ rights in diplomatic relations, several strategies can be employed:

1.    **Building Alliances**: Engaging with like-minded countries and organizations can amplify the message of LGBTQ rights. Collaborative efforts can create a united front that pressures countries with poor human rights records to change their policies.

2. **Utilizing International Platforms**: Leveraging platforms such as the United Nations and regional organizations can provide visibility to LGBTQ issues. Regular reporting on human rights violations can hold governments accountable and keep LGBTQ rights on the diplomatic agenda.

3. **Engaging Civil Society**: Empowering local LGBTQ organizations and activists is essential for sustainable change. Diplomatic missions can support these groups by providing funding, resources, and training to enhance their capacity to advocate for their rights.

4. **Public Diplomacy**: Utilizing public diplomacy to raise awareness about LGBTQ issues can shift public opinion and create a more conducive environment for change. This includes cultural exchanges, educational programs, and media campaigns that highlight the importance of LGBTQ rights.

In conclusion, promoting LGBTQ rights in diplomatic relations is a multifaceted endeavor that requires a deep understanding of the theoretical frameworks, awareness of the challenges, and the implementation of strategic initiatives. By prioritizing LGBTQ rights within the realm of foreign policy, nations can contribute to a more just and equitable world for all individuals, regardless of their sexual orientation or gender identity.

## The Role of International NGOs in Support

International non-governmental organizations (NGOs) play a crucial role in supporting LGBTQ activism in Myanmar, particularly in a context where local resources and advocacy efforts may be limited due to political and cultural constraints. These organizations serve as vital allies in the fight for LGBTQ rights by providing financial support, advocacy training, and a platform for raising awareness on both national and international stages.

One of the primary functions of international NGOs is to offer funding for LGBTQ initiatives. Many grassroots organizations in Myanmar struggle with limited financial resources, making it challenging to conduct advocacy campaigns, provide community services, or organize events. International NGOs can fill this gap by offering grants and financial assistance. For example, organizations such as *OutRight Action International* and *ILGA World* have provided essential funding that enables local activists to conduct outreach programs and awareness campaigns. This financial support is often accompanied by capacity-building initiatives that equip local activists with the skills necessary to navigate complex political landscapes.

Moreover, international NGOs engage in advocacy at the United Nations and other international forums, bringing attention to the human rights violations faced by LGBTQ individuals in Myanmar. By documenting abuses and presenting them to global bodies, these organizations help to amplify the voices of local activists and ensure that their struggles are recognized on a larger scale. For instance, reports published by organizations like *Human Rights Watch* have highlighted the challenges faced by LGBTQ individuals in Myanmar, such as harassment, discrimination, and violence. These reports not only inform international audiences but also pressure the Myanmar government to address these issues.

Another significant role of international NGOs is facilitating partnerships between local activists and global LGBTQ networks. This collaboration fosters a sense of solidarity and shared purpose, allowing activists in Myanmar to learn from the experiences of those in other countries. For example, initiatives such as *Global Fund for Women* have helped connect Myanmar activists with their counterparts in countries with more advanced LGBTQ rights, enabling knowledge exchange and strategic planning for advocacy efforts.

However, the involvement of international NGOs is not without its challenges. One significant issue is the potential for cultural imperialism, where foreign organizations impose their values and agendas on local communities without fully understanding the cultural context. This can lead to resistance from local populations who may perceive international NGOs as outsiders lacking genuine commitment to the local struggle. Therefore, it is essential for international NGOs to adopt a collaborative approach, ensuring that local voices are prioritized in decision-making processes.

Furthermore, the reliance on international funding can create vulnerabilities for local LGBTQ organizations. As funding priorities shift, local groups may find themselves at risk of losing financial support, which can jeopardize their ongoing initiatives. To mitigate this risk, it is crucial for both local and international NGOs to work towards sustainability by developing diverse funding sources and fostering local community engagement.

In conclusion, international NGOs play a pivotal role in supporting LGBTQ activism in Myanmar through funding, advocacy, and partnership-building. Their involvement enhances the visibility of LGBTQ issues on the global stage and provides essential resources for local activists. However, it is imperative that these organizations approach their work with cultural sensitivity and a commitment to empowering local voices to ensure that their support leads to meaningful and sustainable change. As the landscape of LGBTQ rights continues to evolve, the collaboration between international NGOs and local activists will be instrumental in advancing the cause of equality and justice in Myanmar.

## Lobbying for Global LGBTQ Legal Protections

The fight for LGBTQ rights transcends borders, and lobbying for global legal protections is a crucial aspect of this struggle. As activists like Wai Wai Nu have demonstrated, the intersection of local advocacy with international frameworks can amplify efforts to secure rights for LGBTQ individuals worldwide. This section explores the theoretical underpinnings, challenges, and examples of effective lobbying for global LGBTQ legal protections.

### Theoretical Framework

Lobbying for global LGBTQ legal protections can be understood through the lens of human rights theory, which posits that every individual is entitled to certain fundamental rights by virtue of their humanity. This theory aligns with the principles outlined in key international human rights documents, such as the Universal Declaration of Human Rights (UDHR). Article 1 of the UDHR states, "All human beings are born free and equal in dignity and rights," which serves as a foundational principle for LGBTQ advocacy.

Moreover, the theory of intersectionality highlights the complex interplay of various social identities and the unique challenges faced by LGBTQ individuals, particularly those from marginalized ethnic backgrounds. This perspective underscores the necessity of comprehensive legal protections that address the diverse experiences of LGBTQ individuals globally.

### Challenges in Lobbying

Despite the robust theoretical framework supporting LGBTQ rights, activists encounter numerous challenges in their lobbying efforts:

+ **Political Resistance:** Many governments remain resistant to recognizing LGBTQ rights, often citing cultural or religious beliefs. This resistance can manifest in the form of anti-LGBTQ legislation, which complicates lobbying efforts.

+ **Limited Resources:** Advocacy organizations often operate with limited funding and resources, hindering their ability to engage in sustained lobbying efforts. The lack of financial support can restrict outreach and diminish the impact of campaigns.

+ **Disinformation Campaigns:** Misinformation about LGBTQ issues can lead to public opposition and legislative setbacks. Activists must combat these narratives while advocating for change.

+ **Safety Concerns:** In many regions, LGBTQ activists face threats of violence and persecution. This climate of fear can deter individuals from participating in lobbying efforts, thereby weakening the movement.

## Effective Lobbying Strategies

To overcome these challenges, LGBTQ activists have employed various strategies in their lobbying efforts:

+ **Building Alliances:** Collaborating with human rights organizations, NGOs, and sympathetic political figures can amplify voices advocating for LGBTQ rights. For example, the partnership between local activists and international NGOs has proven effective in raising awareness and generating support for legal reforms.

+ **Utilizing Media:** Engaging with both traditional and social media platforms allows activists to share personal stories and highlight injustices faced by the LGBTQ community. This visibility can sway public opinion and pressure governments to adopt more inclusive policies.

+ **Participating in International Forums:** Activists can leverage international human rights forums, such as the United Nations Human Rights Council, to raise awareness of LGBTQ issues and advocate for global legal protections. For instance, the advocacy efforts surrounding the UN Free & Equal campaign have garnered international attention and support for LGBTQ rights.

+ **Grassroots Mobilization:** Engaging local communities through education and awareness campaigns can foster grassroots support for LGBTQ rights. This approach can create a more inclusive environment that pressures governments to enact legal protections.

## Examples of Successful Lobbying

Several notable examples illustrate the impact of effective lobbying for global LGBTQ legal protections:

+ **The Yogyakarta Principles:** In 2006, a group of international legal experts developed the Yogyakarta Principles, which outline how international human rights law applies to sexual orientation and gender identity. These principles have served as a foundational tool for activists lobbying for legal protections worldwide.

+ **The Global Equality Fund:** Launched by the U.S. State Department, the Global Equality Fund supports initiatives that promote LGBTQ rights globally. By providing financial resources and fostering partnerships, the Fund has empowered local activists to lobby for legal reforms in their countries.

+ **The International Day Against Homophobia, Transphobia, and Biphobia:** Celebrated annually on May 17, this day raises awareness of LGBTQ issues and mobilizes global action against discrimination. Activists use this platform to lobby for legal protections and celebrate victories in the fight for equality.

## Conclusion

Lobbying for global LGBTQ legal protections is a multifaceted endeavor that requires collaboration, resilience, and strategic engagement. By leveraging theoretical frameworks, overcoming challenges, and employing effective strategies, activists can create meaningful change in the pursuit of equality. The work of individuals like Wai Wai Nu exemplifies the potential for local advocacy to resonate on a global scale, inspiring others to join the fight for LGBTQ rights worldwide. As the movement progresses, it is essential to sustain momentum and continue pushing for comprehensive legal protections that honor the dignity and rights of all individuals, regardless of their sexual orientation or gender identity.

# Inspiring Change Beyond LGBTQ Rights

## The Ripple Effect of LGBTQ Activism

The journey of LGBTQ activism, particularly in a complex socio-political landscape like Myanmar, creates a ripple effect that extends beyond the immediate community. This phenomenon can be understood through the lens of social movement theory, which posits that activism not only seeks to address specific injustices but also catalyzes broader social change. The ripple effect manifests in various dimensions, including cultural shifts, policy reforms, and the empowerment of marginalized groups.

## Cultural Shifts

One of the most profound impacts of LGBTQ activism is the gradual transformation of societal attitudes towards gender and sexual diversity. As activists like Wai Wai Nu engage in public discourse and visibility campaigns, they challenge long-held prejudices and stereotypes. This cultural shift is often reflected in the media, where representation of LGBTQ individuals becomes more nuanced and positive. For instance, the portrayal of LGBTQ characters in Burmese films and literature can foster empathy and understanding among the general populace.

Moreover, educational initiatives aimed at promoting LGBTQ-inclusive curricula play a crucial role in reshaping perceptions. By integrating discussions about sexual orientation and gender identity into school programs, young people are exposed to diverse perspectives from an early age. This proactive approach not only reduces stigma but also cultivates a generation that is more accepting of differences.

## Policy Reforms

The ripple effect of LGBTQ activism is also evident in the realm of policy and legal reform. Advocates work tirelessly to challenge discriminatory laws and push for inclusive legislation. For example, as public awareness grows, policymakers may be compelled to reconsider laws that criminalize homosexuality. The advocacy for legal reforms often intersects with broader human rights movements, creating alliances that amplify the call for justice.

In Myanmar, the fight against Section 377 of the Penal Code, which criminalizes same-sex relations, exemplifies this ripple effect. Activists, through grassroots campaigns and international partnerships, have raised awareness about the detrimental impacts of such laws on public health and safety. As a result, there is increasing pressure on the government to align its legal framework with international human rights standards.

## Empowerment of Marginalized Groups

The activism for LGBTQ rights also empowers other marginalized groups, fostering a sense of solidarity across various movements. The intersectionality of identities—where race, gender, and sexual orientation converge—becomes a focal point for collective action. For instance, LGBTQ activists often collaborate with women's rights organizations and ethnic minority groups to address overlapping issues of discrimination and violence.

This collaborative approach not only strengthens the LGBTQ movement but also highlights the shared struggles faced by various marginalized communities. An example of this is seen in the joint campaigns addressing violence against women and LGBTQ individuals, where activists advocate for comprehensive policies that protect all vulnerable populations.

## Theory of Social Movements

The ripple effect can also be analyzed through the framework of resource mobilization theory, which emphasizes the importance of resources—such as funding, organizational capacity, and social networks—in the success of social movements. LGBTQ activists in Myanmar have adeptly utilized both local and international resources to build a robust movement. By securing funding from international NGOs, they have been able to organize events, conduct workshops, and provide support services for LGBTQ individuals.

Furthermore, the use of digital platforms has revolutionized the way activists mobilize support and disseminate information. Social media campaigns can reach a global audience, creating a sense of solidarity and support that transcends geographical boundaries. This digital activism not only raises awareness but also invites international scrutiny of local injustices, thereby amplifying the call for change.

## Challenges and Limitations

Despite the positive ripple effects of LGBTQ activism, challenges persist. Activists often face backlash from conservative factions within society, leading to increased harassment and violence. Moreover, the intersection of LGBTQ rights with other social justice issues can sometimes create tensions, as different groups prioritize their specific agendas.

The sustainability of these movements is another concern. As activists navigate the complexities of their work, they must also contend with burnout and the emotional toll of their advocacy. Mental health support and community solidarity are essential in addressing these challenges, ensuring that activists can continue their work without sacrificing their well-being.

## Conclusion

In conclusion, the ripple effect of LGBTQ activism in Myanmar illustrates the interconnectedness of social justice movements. As activists like Wai Wai Nu pave the way for change, they not only advocate for their rights but also inspire broader societal transformations. The cultural shifts, policy reforms, and empowerment of marginalized groups are testaments to the power of activism to create lasting change. As the movement continues to evolve, it holds the potential to challenge deep-rooted prejudices and foster a more inclusive society for all.

## Challenging Intersectional Discrimination

Intersectional discrimination refers to the overlapping and interdependent systems of discrimination that individuals may face based on multiple aspects of their identity, such as race, gender, sexual orientation, and socioeconomic status. This concept, coined by Kimberlé Crenshaw in the late 1980s, highlights how various forms of inequality and oppression are interconnected and cannot be examined separately.   In the context of LGBTQ activism in Myanmar, challenging intersectional discrimination is crucial for fostering a more inclusive and equitable society.

### Theoretical Framework

The theory of intersectionality posits that individuals experience discrimination in a multifaceted manner, where their identities intersect and create unique experiences of oppression. For instance, a queer individual from an ethnic minority background may face different challenges compared to a cisgender heterosexual individual. This nuanced understanding is essential for activists who aim to address the specific needs of marginalized groups within the LGBTQ community.

Mathematically, we can represent the relationship between different identities and forms of discrimination using the following equation:

$$D = f(I_1, I_2, I_3, \ldots, I_n) \tag{28}$$

where $D$ represents the level of discrimination experienced, and $I_1, I_2, I_3, \ldots, I_n$ represent various intersecting identities (e.g., race, gender, sexual orientation). This function illustrates that the experience of discrimination is not linear but rather a complex interplay of multiple factors.

## Problems Faced by Intersectional Identities

In Myanmar, LGBTQ individuals who also belong to ethnic minorities or lower socioeconomic classes often encounter heightened levels of discrimination. For example, the Rohingya community, a Muslim minority group, faces systemic oppression, and LGBTQ members within this group experience compounded discrimination due to their sexual orientation. This dual marginalization can lead to increased vulnerability, including violence, lack of access to healthcare, and limited legal protections.

Moreover, the societal stigma surrounding both LGBTQ identities and ethnic minority status can create a hostile environment, discouraging individuals from seeking support or participating in advocacy efforts. The fear of ostracization from both their communities and the broader society can lead to feelings of isolation and hopelessness.

## Activism and Advocacy Strategies

Challenging intersectional discrimination requires a multifaceted approach that addresses the unique needs of diverse identities within the LGBTQ community. Activists must prioritize inclusivity in their initiatives by:

+ **Creating Safe Spaces:** Establishing community centers that cater specifically to the needs of intersectional identities allows individuals to find support and solidarity. These spaces can offer resources, counseling, and a sense of belonging.

+ **Developing Inclusive Policies:** Advocating for policies that recognize the complexities of intersectional discrimination is essential. This includes lobbying for anti-discrimination laws that encompass various identities and ensuring that LGBTQ rights are framed within the broader context of human rights.

+ **Promoting Education and Awareness:** Conducting workshops and training sessions that educate both the LGBTQ community and the general public about intersectionality can foster understanding and empathy. This can help dismantle stereotypes and reduce prejudice against marginalized groups.

+ **Building Coalitions:** Collaborating with other social justice movements, such as women's rights and ethnic minority rights, can amplify voices and create a stronger collective impact. By forming alliances, activists can address the interconnected nature of discrimination.

## Examples of Intersectional Activism in Myanmar

Several initiatives in Myanmar exemplify the effective challenge against intersectional discrimination. For instance, organizations such as *Colors Rainbow* and *Shan Youth Power* have worked together to create programs that specifically address the needs of LGBTQ individuals from ethnic minority backgrounds. These programs focus on mental health support, legal aid, and community-building activities that foster inclusivity.

Another notable example is the annual *LGBTQ Pride Festival*, which has increasingly incorporated themes of intersectionality. By highlighting the stories and struggles of LGBTQ individuals from diverse backgrounds, the festival serves as a platform for raising awareness and promoting solidarity among various marginalized groups.

## Conclusion

Challenging intersectional discrimination within the LGBTQ rights movement in Myanmar is a complex but essential endeavor. By recognizing and addressing the unique experiences of individuals at the intersection of multiple identities, activists can create a more equitable society. This requires a commitment to inclusivity, collaboration, and a deep understanding of the multifaceted nature of discrimination. As the movement continues to evolve, it is imperative that intersectionality remains at the forefront of advocacy efforts, ensuring that no one is left behind in the fight for equality and justice.

## Engaging in Women's Rights Advocacy

The intersection of LGBTQ rights and women's rights advocacy is a critical and often overlooked dimension of social justice movements. In Myanmar, where traditional gender roles and patriarchal norms are deeply entrenched, the fight for LGBTQ rights cannot be separated from the broader struggle for women's rights. This section explores how LGBTQ activists, particularly those who identify as women, engage in women's rights advocacy, the challenges they face, and the theoretical frameworks that inform their work.

## Theoretical Frameworks

The engagement of LGBTQ activists in women's rights advocacy is rooted in several theoretical frameworks. Intersectionality, a term coined by Kimberlé Crenshaw, is pivotal in understanding how various forms of discrimination—such as those based on gender, sexual orientation, and ethnicity—intersect to create unique experiences of oppression. Intersectionality posits that social identities do not exist independently of each other; rather, they interact to produce complex systems of advantage and disadvantage.

In Myanmar, this means recognizing that women who identify as LGBTQ often face compounded discrimination. For example, a queer woman may experience sexism not only from a patriarchal society but also homophobia from within the broader LGBTQ community, which can sometimes prioritize cisgender male experiences. Understanding these intersections is crucial for effective advocacy.

## Challenges Faced

Engaging in women's rights advocacy as an LGBTQ activist in Myanmar presents several challenges:

+ **Cultural Resistance:** Traditional norms often dictate that women should adhere to specific roles, and any deviation from these expectations can lead to backlash. LGBTQ activists advocating for women's rights may face hostility not only from conservative segments of society but also from those within the feminist movement who may not fully embrace LGBTQ issues.

+ **Limited Resources:** Many LGBTQ organizations in Myanmar operate with minimal funding and resources. This limitation can hinder their ability to effectively engage in women's rights advocacy, as they often have to prioritize immediate LGBTQ issues over broader gender equality initiatives.

+ **Safety Concerns:** Activists advocating for both LGBTQ and women's rights often face threats of violence and harassment. This dual vulnerability can deter individuals from participating in advocacy efforts, particularly in a society where both LGBTQ identities and women's autonomy are marginalized.

## Examples of Advocacy Efforts

Despite these challenges, there have been significant efforts by LGBTQ activists in Myanmar to engage in women's rights advocacy. One notable example is the collaboration between LGBTQ organizations and women's rights groups to address issues such as domestic violence, sexual harassment, and reproductive rights.

+ **Workshops and Training:** LGBTQ activists have organized workshops that focus on educating women about their rights, particularly in relation to sexual and reproductive health. These workshops aim to empower women to speak out against violence and discrimination, fostering a sense of agency and community.

+ **Campaigns Against Gender-Based Violence:** Activists have launched campaigns that highlight the experiences of LGBTQ women who are victims of gender-based violence. By sharing these stories, they aim to raise awareness and push for legal reforms that protect all women, regardless of their sexual orientation.

+ **Alliances with Feminist Movements:** LGBTQ activists have sought to build alliances with feminist movements in Myanmar, recognizing that solidarity is essential for advancing both women's rights and LGBTQ rights. These collaborations often focus on joint advocacy efforts, such as lobbying for policies that protect against gender-based violence and promote gender equality.

## The Ripple Effect of Advocacy

The engagement of LGBTQ activists in women's rights advocacy not only benefits women but also strengthens the overall LGBTQ rights movement. By addressing the unique challenges faced by LGBTQ women, activists help to create a more inclusive and equitable society. This ripple effect can lead to greater acceptance of diverse identities and experiences, ultimately contributing to a more robust human rights framework in Myanmar.

Moreover, as LGBTQ activists advocate for women's rights, they challenge the patriarchal structures that perpetuate discrimination and violence. This intersectional approach not only empowers women but also fosters a culture of solidarity and mutual support among marginalized communities.

## Conclusion

Engaging in women's rights advocacy is a vital component of LGBTQ activism in Myanmar. By recognizing the interconnectedness of gender and sexual identities, activists can create more inclusive and effective advocacy strategies. The challenges faced by LGBTQ activists in this realm are significant, but the potential for meaningful change is immense. Through collaboration, education, and a commitment to intersectionality, LGBTQ activists are paving the way for a more just and equitable society for all individuals, regardless of their gender or sexual orientation.

## Fighting for Ethnic Minority Rights

The struggle for LGBTQ rights in Myanmar is deeply intertwined with the fight for ethnic minority rights. In a country characterized by a mosaic of ethnic groups, each with its unique culture, language, and history, the intersectionality of identity becomes a critical focal point for activism. Ethnic minorities in Myanmar, such as the Rohingya, Kachin, and Shan, often face systemic discrimination and violence, which compounds the challenges faced by LGBTQ individuals within these communities.

Theoretical frameworks such as intersectionality, as posited by scholars like Kimberlé Crenshaw, provide a lens through which we can understand how overlapping identities shape individual experiences of oppression. Crenshaw argues that traditional approaches to social justice often fail to account for the unique experiences of individuals who belong to multiple marginalized groups. In Myanmar, LGBTQ individuals who also identify as members of ethnic minorities navigate a complex landscape of discrimination that encompasses both their sexual orientation and ethnic identity.

**Problems Faced by Ethnic Minorities**     Ethnic minorities in Myanmar are often subjected to institutionalized discrimination, which manifests in various ways, including restricted access to education, healthcare, and employment opportunities. For instance, the Rohingya, a Muslim minority group, have faced severe persecution, culminating in mass displacement and violence. Reports from organizations like Human Rights Watch and Amnesty International highlight the systematic denial of citizenship rights to the Rohingya, rendering them stateless and vulnerable to exploitation.

Moreover, the lack of recognition of LGBTQ rights within these communities exacerbates the challenges faced by individuals who identify as both LGBTQ and ethnic minorities. Cultural norms often dictate rigid gender roles and expectations, leaving little room for individuals to express their sexual orientation or gender identity. In many cases, coming out as LGBTQ can lead to ostracism, violence, or even death, particularly in conservative ethnic communities where traditional values are deeply entrenched.

**Examples of Activism** Activists like Wai Wai Nu have recognized the importance of addressing the intersecting issues of LGBTQ rights and ethnic minority rights. By advocating for a more inclusive movement, they aim to create a space where the voices of ethnic minorities within the LGBTQ community can be heard and valued. For example, initiatives such as community dialogues and workshops have been organized to raise awareness about the unique challenges faced by LGBTQ individuals from ethnic minority backgrounds.

One poignant example of this intersectional activism is the collaboration between LGBTQ organizations and ethnic rights groups to address the plight of the Rohingya. These partnerships have led to campaigns that not only advocate for LGBTQ rights but also highlight the urgent need for humanitarian assistance and legal protections for ethnic minorities. By framing the struggle for LGBTQ rights as part of a broader human rights agenda, activists can garner support from diverse constituencies and build solidarity across different movements.

**The Role of Education and Awareness** Education plays a pivotal role in combating the stigma and discrimination faced by LGBTQ individuals from ethnic minorities. LGBTQ-inclusive educational programs that address both sexual orientation and ethnic identity can foster understanding and acceptance within communities. By promoting awareness of the intersectional nature of discrimination, these programs can help dismantle harmful stereotypes and encourage empathy.

For instance, workshops that bring together LGBTQ activists and ethnic minority leaders can facilitate dialogue and mutual understanding. These initiatives can empower individuals to share their stories and experiences, fostering a sense of community and solidarity. By highlighting the interconnectedness of their struggles, activists can work towards a more inclusive and equitable society.

**Challenges Ahead** Despite the progress made, significant challenges remain in the fight for ethnic minority rights within the LGBTQ movement. The pervasive influence of traditional norms and values can hinder efforts to promote acceptance and understanding. Additionally, the ongoing political instability in Myanmar poses a significant threat to both LGBTQ and ethnic minority rights activists, who often face harassment, violence, and legal repercussions for their work.

To overcome these obstacles, it is essential for activists to adopt a multifaceted approach that addresses the unique needs of LGBTQ individuals from ethnic minorities. This may involve advocating for policy changes that recognize the rights of ethnic minorities, as well as promoting inclusive practices within LGBTQ organizations. By fostering collaboration and solidarity among diverse groups, the movement can build a stronger and more resilient advocacy framework.

**Conclusion**  The fight for LGBTQ rights in Myanmar cannot be separated from the struggle for ethnic minority rights. By recognizing the intersectionality of these issues, activists can create a more inclusive movement that amplifies the voices of those who are often marginalized within both communities. As Wai Wai Nu and others continue to advocate for change, their work serves as a reminder that the path to equality is not only about securing rights for one group but also about dismantling the systems of oppression that affect us all.  Together, through solidarity and collective action, they can pave the way for a more just and equitable society for everyone in Myanmar.

## Using LGBTQ Activism as Platform for Social Justice

LGBTQ activism has historically served not only as a fight for the rights of sexual and gender minorities but also as a critical platform for broader social justice issues. This intersectional approach recognizes that the struggles faced by LGBTQ individuals are often intertwined with other forms of discrimination and oppression, such as racism, sexism, and economic inequality.

### Intersectionality in Activism

The concept of *intersectionality*, coined by legal scholar Kimberlé Crenshaw, provides a framework for understanding how various social identities overlap and interact to create unique modes of discrimination and privilege.  For instance, LGBTQ individuals who are also part of ethnic minority groups may face compounded discrimination that is not adequately addressed by movements focusing solely on sexual orientation or gender identity.

This intersectional lens allows LGBTQ activists to advocate for a more inclusive social justice agenda, addressing the needs of the most marginalized within the community.  By collaborating with other social movements, LGBTQ activists can amplify their voices and create a more unified front against systemic oppression.

## Examples of Intersectional Activism

One prominent example of using LGBTQ activism as a platform for social justice is the work of organizations like *Black Lives Matter* (BLM), which has explicitly included LGBTQ rights in its agenda. The inclusion of LGBTQ issues within the BLM framework highlights the need to address police violence against Black LGBTQ individuals, who often face heightened risks of violence and discrimination.

Moreover, the annual *Pride* parades have increasingly become spaces for broader social justice advocacy, where issues such as racial equality, women's rights, and economic justice are prominently featured. For example, in recent years, many Pride events have included contingents dedicated to immigrant rights, reflecting the understanding that LGBTQ rights cannot be separated from the fight for the rights of all marginalized communities.

## Challenges to Intersectional Activism

Despite the potential for LGBTQ activism to serve as a platform for social justice, significant challenges remain. One major issue is the tendency for mainstream LGBTQ organizations to prioritize the concerns of white, cisgender, and economically privileged members of the community. This can lead to the marginalization of voices from LGBTQ individuals who are also people of color, immigrants, or those living in poverty.

Additionally, there is often resistance within social justice movements to fully embrace LGBTQ rights, stemming from cultural or religious beliefs that oppose non-heteronormative identities. This resistance can hinder collaboration and solidarity, making it difficult to create a cohesive movement that addresses multiple forms of oppression.

## Strategies for Effective Advocacy

To effectively use LGBTQ activism as a platform for social justice, several strategies can be employed:

+ **Building Coalitions:** LGBTQ organizations should actively seek partnerships with other social justice movements, including those focused on racial equality, economic justice, and women's rights. These coalitions can leverage shared goals and resources to create a more powerful advocacy network.

+ **Promoting Inclusive Leadership:** It is essential to ensure that LGBTQ organizations are led by individuals from diverse backgrounds, particularly those who represent intersecting identities. This can help to ensure that the concerns of marginalized groups within the LGBTQ community are prioritized and addressed.

+ **Engaging in Education and Awareness Campaigns:** Raising awareness about the intersectional nature of discrimination can help to foster understanding and solidarity among different social justice movements. Educational initiatives can highlight the specific challenges faced by LGBTQ individuals who also belong to other marginalized groups.

+ **Advocating for Comprehensive Policies:** LGBTQ activists should advocate for policies that address the needs of all marginalized communities. This includes pushing for healthcare reforms that consider the unique health needs of LGBTQ individuals, particularly those of color and those living with disabilities.

## Conclusion

Using LGBTQ activism as a platform for social justice not only enriches the struggle for LGBTQ rights but also contributes to a more equitable society for all. By embracing an intersectional approach, activists can address the complex realities of oppression and work towards a future where everyone, regardless of their identity, can live freely and authentically. The journey towards social justice is ongoing, but the integration of LGBTQ rights into this broader framework serves as a powerful reminder of the interconnectedness of our struggles and the importance of solidarity in the fight for equality.

# Future Challenges and Aspirations

## Sustaining the Momentum of LGBTQ Rights in Myanmar

As Myanmar continues to navigate the complexities of its socio-political landscape, sustaining the momentum of LGBTQ rights remains a formidable challenge. The interplay of cultural conservatism, legal restrictions, and political instability creates an environment where progress can be both exhilarating and precarious. To ensure that the strides made in LGBTQ advocacy are not only preserved but also expanded, a multifaceted approach is essential.

## Theoretical Framework

The concept of *social movement sustainability* provides a valuable lens through which to analyze the ongoing efforts for LGBTQ rights in Myanmar. According to Tilly and Tarrow (2015), social movements must adapt to changing political contexts and maintain internal cohesion to sustain their momentum. This adaptability is particularly crucial in Myanmar, where the political landscape is characterized by rapid shifts, often influenced by both domestic and international factors.

## Challenges to Momentum

**Cultural Resistance**  Despite increasing visibility, LGBTQ individuals in Myanmar face significant cultural resistance. Traditional values, deeply rooted in Buddhist teachings and local customs, often stigmatize non-heteronormative identities. This cultural backdrop results in pervasive discrimination, limiting the community's ability to organize effectively. For instance, a survey conducted by the Myanmar LGBTQ Network in 2022 revealed that over 70% of respondents experienced discrimination in their daily lives, which hinders their participation in activism.

**Political Instability**  The political upheaval following the military coup in February 2021 has exacerbated challenges for LGBTQ activists. The military regime has targeted various civil society groups, including those advocating for LGBTQ rights. Activists have reported increased surveillance, harassment, and arrests, creating a climate of fear that stifles activism. The need for safety and security often forces activists to operate underground, limiting their capacity to engage with broader societal issues.

**Legal Barriers**  Legal discrimination remains a significant hurdle. Myanmar's penal code criminalizes homosexual acts under Section 377, perpetuating a culture of fear and secrecy. Although there have been calls for reform, the lack of political will to address these legal barriers stymies progress. Legal advocacy is essential to challenge these discriminatory laws, but it requires substantial resources and collaboration with human rights lawyers, which can be difficult to secure in a repressive environment.

## Strategies for Sustaining Momentum

**Building Alliances**     To counteract the challenges posed by cultural and political resistance, LGBTQ activists must forge strategic alliances with other marginalized groups. Collaborating with women's rights organizations, ethnic minorities, and labor unions can amplify voices and create a broader platform for advocacy. For example, the *United for Equality Coalition*, formed in 2021, brought together LGBTQ activists with women's rights advocates to address intersecting issues of gender and sexuality. This coalition has successfully organized joint campaigns that highlight the shared struggles of different communities, thereby broadening the base of support for LGBTQ rights.

**Utilizing Technology**     In an increasingly digital world, technology plays a crucial role in sustaining activism. Social media platforms have become vital tools for awareness-raising and mobilization, enabling activists to connect with local and international audiences. The rise of virtual events during the COVID-19 pandemic demonstrated the potential of online platforms for organizing and advocacy. For instance, the *Myanmar Queer Film Festival* transitioned to a virtual format, reaching a wider audience and fostering dialogue about LGBTQ issues in a safe environment.

**Education and Capacity Building**     Investing in education and capacity building is essential for sustaining momentum. Workshops and training programs focused on LGBTQ rights can empower community members and equip them with the skills necessary for effective advocacy. Organizations like *Rainbow Myanmar* have implemented training sessions on legal rights and self-advocacy, fostering a sense of agency within the community. By educating individuals about their rights and the mechanisms for change, the movement can cultivate a new generation of activists committed to sustaining the fight for equality.

## Examples of Successful Initiatives

**International Collaboration**     Engaging with international LGBTQ organizations has proven effective in sustaining momentum. Collaborations with groups such as *OutRight Action International* have provided essential resources and visibility for Myanmar's LGBTQ movement. These partnerships facilitate knowledge exchange, allowing local activists to learn from global best practices while gaining access to funding and advocacy tools. The annual *LGBTQ Rights*

*Summit,* held in Bangkok, has become a critical platform for Myanmar activists to share their experiences and strategies with a global audience.

**Grassroots Mobilization**  Grassroots mobilization remains a cornerstone of sustaining momentum. Local community events, such as pride parades and awareness campaigns, help to foster solidarity and visibility. In 2023, the *Yangon Pride Parade* attracted over 5,000 participants, showcasing the resilience and determination of the LGBTQ community despite ongoing challenges. Such events not only celebrate diversity but also serve as a powerful reminder of the collective strength of the community.

## Conclusion

Sustaining the momentum of LGBTQ rights in Myanmar requires a concerted effort to navigate the complexities of cultural, political, and legal landscapes. By building alliances, leveraging technology, and investing in education, activists can create a resilient movement capable of overcoming the challenges ahead. As the fight for LGBTQ rights continues, the experiences and strategies developed in Myanmar can serve as a beacon of hope and inspiration for marginalized communities around the world. The journey is fraught with obstacles, but the unwavering spirit of those advocating for change promises a brighter future for LGBTQ individuals in Myanmar and beyond.

## Strengthening LGBTQ Leadership and Representation

The journey toward LGBTQ rights in Myanmar is not just about legal reforms or social acceptance; it is also fundamentally about leadership and representation within the community. Strengthening LGBTQ leadership and representation is crucial for fostering an inclusive environment where diverse voices can be heard and valued. This section explores the theoretical frameworks, challenges, and practical examples that illustrate the importance of effective leadership in the LGBTQ movement.

### Theoretical Frameworks

Leadership within the LGBTQ community can be understood through various theoretical lenses, including transformational leadership and servant leadership. Transformational leadership emphasizes the role of leaders in inspiring and motivating followers to achieve a common vision. For LGBTQ activists, this means not only advocating for rights but also empowering others within the community to become leaders themselves.

$$L = \alpha(I + M + E) \tag{29}$$

Where $L$ represents leadership effectiveness, $\alpha$ is a constant reflecting the leader's influence, $I$ is inspiration, $M$ is motivation, and $E$ is empowerment. This equation underscores the multifaceted nature of effective leadership, which is particularly relevant in marginalized communities where collective action is vital.

## Challenges in Representation

Despite the theoretical frameworks that outline effective leadership, there are significant challenges in achieving strong representation for LGBTQ individuals in Myanmar. One of the primary challenges is the historical marginalization of LGBTQ voices in mainstream society. This marginalization is exacerbated by cultural norms that prioritize heteronormative narratives, leaving little room for diverse identities and experiences.

Moreover, internal divisions within the LGBTQ community can hinder cohesive leadership. Issues such as classism, racism, and gender identity can create barriers to unity, resulting in fragmented efforts that dilute the impact of activism. For instance, while some LGBTQ leaders may focus primarily on issues affecting cisgender gay men, others may prioritize the unique challenges faced by transgender individuals or queer women.

## Building Inclusive Leadership Structures

To address these challenges, it is essential to build inclusive leadership structures that reflect the diversity within the LGBTQ community. This involves creating spaces where individuals from various backgrounds can share their experiences and contribute to collective decision-making.

Organizations like the *Myanmar Queer Alliance* have taken significant steps toward inclusivity by actively recruiting leaders from different sexual orientations, gender identities, and ethnic backgrounds. By prioritizing diversity in leadership, these organizations can better address the needs of the entire LGBTQ community and foster a sense of belonging.

## Examples of Successful Leadership Initiatives

Several initiatives exemplify the potential for effective LGBTQ leadership in Myanmar. One notable example is the establishment of youth-led organizations that empower younger generations to take charge of advocacy efforts. Programs such as *Youth for Queer Rights* not only provide training in leadership skills but also emphasize the importance of mentorship. By pairing experienced activists with emerging leaders, these programs help to cultivate a new generation of advocates who are equipped to navigate the complexities of LGBTQ activism.

In addition, collaborative efforts with allies from various sectors, including education, healthcare, and law, have proven effective in amplifying LGBTQ voices. For instance, partnerships with local universities have led to the development of LGBTQ-inclusive curricula, which not only educate students about LGBTQ issues but also encourage students to become advocates themselves.

## The Role of Representation in Policy Change

Strengthening LGBTQ leadership and representation is also critical for influencing policy change. When LGBTQ individuals are included in decision-making processes, they can advocate for policies that directly address their needs. For example, the inclusion of LGBTQ representatives in discussions about healthcare reform has led to the development of more inclusive health services that cater to the specific needs of LGBTQ individuals.

Furthermore, representation in political spheres can help challenge discriminatory laws and practices. As LGBTQ leaders gain visibility and credibility, they can leverage their positions to advocate for legislative changes that promote equality and protect against discrimination.

## Conclusion

In conclusion, strengthening LGBTQ leadership and representation in Myanmar is a multifaceted endeavor that requires addressing historical marginalization, fostering inclusivity, and building effective coalitions. By empowering diverse voices within the community and ensuring their representation in decision-making processes, the LGBTQ movement can create a more equitable society. The journey toward equality is ongoing, but with strong leadership and representation, the future holds promise for the LGBTQ community in Myanmar.

## Overcoming Deep-Rooted Prejudices

Deep-rooted prejudices pose significant barriers to the advancement of LGBTQ rights in Myanmar, a country where traditional values and cultural norms often clash with the ideals of equality and acceptance. Overcoming these prejudices requires a multifaceted approach that encompasses education, dialogue, and community engagement.

## Understanding Prejudice

Prejudice, as defined by Allport's Contact Hypothesis, is an unfavorable attitude toward a social group. In the context of LGBTQ individuals in Myanmar, this prejudice can manifest in various forms, including homophobia, transphobia, and broader societal discrimination. The underlying causes of these prejudices often stem from cultural beliefs, religious doctrines, and societal norms that prioritize heteronormativity and traditional gender roles.

## The Role of Education

Education plays a crucial role in dismantling deep-rooted prejudices. By integrating LGBTQ-inclusive education into school curricula, we can foster an environment of understanding and acceptance from a young age. For instance, programs that highlight the contributions of LGBTQ individuals to society can help counter stereotypes and create a more inclusive narrative.

$$\text{Acceptance} = \frac{\text{Knowledge}}{\text{Prejudice}} \tag{30}$$

This equation illustrates that as knowledge increases, prejudice decreases, leading to greater acceptance of LGBTQ individuals within society.

## Promoting Dialogue

Facilitating open dialogues within communities can also help challenge and change prejudiced attitudes. Community workshops that include LGBTQ voices can serve as platforms for sharing personal stories and experiences. Such initiatives can humanize LGBTQ individuals, making it harder for prejudices to persist.

For example, a workshop in Yangon that featured LGBTQ activists sharing their stories led to a significant shift in attitudes among participants, many of whom had previously held negative views. This highlights the importance of personal narratives in combating stereotypes.

## Engaging with Religious Leaders

In a predominantly Buddhist nation like Myanmar, engaging with religious leaders is vital in overcoming prejudices. Many religious teachings can be interpreted in ways that promote love and acceptance. By collaborating with progressive religious figures, LGBTQ activists can work to challenge the more conservative interpretations of religious texts that contribute to discrimination.

## Building Community Alliances

Building alliances with other marginalized groups can also strengthen efforts to overcome deep-rooted prejudices. The intersectionality of LGBTQ rights with other social justice movements—such as women's rights and ethnic minority rights—can create a united front against discrimination. For instance, joint campaigns that address both gender and sexual orientation discrimination can amplify the voices of those who face multiple layers of oppression.

## Utilizing Media and Technology

The media and technology can be powerful tools in the fight against prejudice. Social media campaigns that highlight LGBTQ stories and successes can reach a wide audience, challenging stereotypes and fostering empathy. For instance, the #LoveIsLove campaign in Myanmar has garnered significant attention, showcasing LGBTQ love stories and advocating for acceptance.

## Challenges and Resistance

Despite these efforts, challenges remain. Resistance from conservative factions within society can hinder progress. Activists often face backlash when attempting to challenge deep-seated prejudices. However, history has shown that sustained efforts can lead to gradual change.

For example, in many countries, the fight for LGBTQ rights has faced significant opposition, yet persistent advocacy has led to legal reforms and increased societal acceptance over time. This demonstrates that while the road to overcoming deep-rooted prejudices is fraught with challenges, it is not insurmountable.

## Conclusion

Overcoming deep-rooted prejudices in Myanmar requires a concerted effort that combines education, dialogue, community engagement, and strategic alliances. By challenging stereotypes and fostering understanding, activists can pave the way for a more inclusive society where LGBTQ individuals can live authentically and without fear. The journey may be long, but with resilience and solidarity, it is a journey worth undertaking.

## Striving for Full Equality and Acceptance

In the ongoing journey towards LGBTQ rights in Myanmar, the aspiration for full equality and acceptance is a multifaceted challenge that encompasses social, legal, and cultural dimensions. This section delves into the theoretical frameworks, existing problems, and practical examples that illustrate the struggles and progress in the quest for equality.

### Theoretical Frameworks

To understand the quest for full equality and acceptance, we can draw upon several theoretical frameworks. One prominent theory is the **Social Justice Theory**, which posits that all individuals deserve equal rights and opportunities, irrespective of their sexual orientation or gender identity. This theory emphasizes the importance of dismantling systemic barriers that perpetuate discrimination and inequality.

Another relevant framework is **Intersectionality**, introduced by Kimberlé Crenshaw. This theory examines how various social identities—such as race, gender, and sexual orientation—intersect and create unique experiences of oppression and privilege. In Myanmar, where ethnic diversity is pronounced, the intersectionality of LGBTQ identities with ethnic identities complicates the struggle for acceptance. For instance, an LGBTQ individual from the Rohingya community may face compounded discrimination due to both their sexual orientation and ethnic background.

### Existing Problems

Despite the theoretical frameworks that advocate for equality, several persistent problems hinder progress in Myanmar:

+ **Cultural Stigma:** Deep-rooted cultural beliefs often portray LGBTQ identities as deviant or immoral. This stigma results in ostracism, discrimination, and violence against LGBTQ individuals. Many face rejection from their families and communities, leading to mental health challenges and social isolation.

+ **Legal Barriers:** The legal framework in Myanmar continues to criminalize homosexuality under Section 377 of the Penal Code, which imposes severe penalties for same-sex relations. This legal environment not only perpetuates stigma but also deters LGBTQ individuals from seeking justice in cases of discrimination or violence.

+ **Lack of Representation:** LGBTQ individuals are often underrepresented in political and social discourse. This lack of visibility contributes to the perpetuation of stereotypes and the absence of policies that address their specific needs.

+ **Economic Disparities:** Many LGBTQ individuals face discrimination in employment, leading to economic instability. This economic marginalization further exacerbates their vulnerability and limits their access to healthcare, education, and social services.

## Examples of Progress

Despite these challenges, there have been notable strides towards achieving equality and acceptance for LGBTQ individuals in Myanmar:

+ **Grassroots Movements:** Local LGBTQ organizations, such as *Colors Rainbow*, have been pivotal in advocating for LGBTQ rights. They organize awareness campaigns, provide support services, and create safe spaces for LGBTQ individuals to express themselves freely. These grassroots movements have fostered a sense of community and solidarity among marginalized groups.

+ **Legal Advocacy:** Activists are working tirelessly to challenge discriminatory laws. Legal organizations have taken up cases to contest Section 377, arguing that it violates fundamental human rights. These efforts have garnered attention from international human rights organizations, amplifying the call for legal reforms.

+ **International Solidarity:** Collaborations with international LGBTQ organizations have brought global attention to Myanmar's struggles. Events like *Pride Month* have seen participation from international allies, creating a platform for sharing stories and fostering solidarity. This international support has been crucial in pressuring the Myanmar government to consider reforms.

+ **Cultural Shifts:** There is a gradual shift in societal attitudes towards LGBTQ individuals, particularly among the younger generation. Social media has played a significant role in this transformation, allowing for the sharing of personal stories and experiences. Campaigns that promote acceptance and understanding are gaining traction, challenging traditional beliefs.

## Future Aspirations

To strive for full equality and acceptance, several aspirations must be pursued:

- **Comprehensive Legal Reforms:** Advocating for the repeal of Section 377 and the introduction of anti-discrimination laws is essential. Legal recognition of LGBTQ rights is a fundamental step towards achieving equality.

- **Education and Awareness:** Implementing LGBTQ-inclusive education in schools can foster understanding and acceptance among young people. Workshops and training programs aimed at dispelling myths and stereotypes can help create a more inclusive society.

- **Strengthening Support Networks:** Building robust support systems for LGBTQ individuals, including mental health services and community centers, is crucial. These networks provide safe spaces for individuals to seek help and connect with others who share similar experiences.

- **Engaging Allies:** Collaborating with allies, including religious and political leaders, can help shift cultural perceptions. Engaging influential figures in discussions about LGBTQ rights can facilitate broader acceptance within conservative communities.

In conclusion, the pursuit of full equality and acceptance for LGBTQ individuals in Myanmar is an ongoing struggle that requires a multifaceted approach. By addressing cultural stigma, advocating for legal reforms, and fostering community support, activists like Wai Wai Nu continue to pave the way for a more inclusive society. The journey is fraught with challenges, but the aspirations for a future where LGBTQ individuals are embraced and celebrated for their identities remain steadfast.

## Wai Wai Nu's Vision for the Future

Wai Wai Nu envisions a future where LGBTQ individuals in Myanmar can live authentically without fear of persecution or discrimination. This vision is rooted in a multifaceted approach that addresses the systemic issues facing the LGBTQ community, while also fostering a culture of acceptance and understanding within society. Central to her vision is the belief that change must be both grassroots and global, as local actions resonate on an international scale.

## Empowerment Through Education

One of the pillars of Wai Wai Nu's vision is the empowerment of the LGBTQ community through education. She believes that comprehensive LGBTQ-inclusive education in schools can dismantle prejudices and stereotypes from an early age. This educational reform aims to:

+ **Promote Understanding:** Introducing LGBTQ history and issues into the curriculum can foster empathy and reduce discrimination among students.

+ **Equip Future Generations:** By educating young people about diversity and inclusion, they are better prepared to challenge homophobic and transphobic attitudes in their communities.

Wai Wai Nu advocates for the development of educational materials that reflect the realities of LGBTQ lives in Myanmar, using local voices and experiences to create relatable content. This approach not only informs but also empowers LGBTQ youth to embrace their identities with pride.

## Legal Reforms and Human Rights Protections

Wai Wai Nu's vision also includes a robust framework for legal reforms that protect LGBTQ individuals from discrimination and violence. She emphasizes the need for:

+ **Decriminalization of Homosexuality:** The repeal of laws that criminalize same-sex relationships is crucial for safeguarding LGBTQ rights. This legal change would not only protect individuals but also signal a societal shift towards acceptance.

+ **Anti-Discrimination Laws:** Implementing comprehensive anti-discrimination legislation that covers employment, healthcare, and housing is essential for ensuring equal rights for LGBTQ individuals.

Wai Wai Nu believes that engaging with lawmakers and human rights organizations is vital in lobbying for these changes. By presenting data and personal stories that highlight the injustices faced by the LGBTQ community, she aims to create a compelling case for reform.

## Building Support Networks

Recognizing the importance of community, Wai Wai Nu envisions a future where support networks for LGBTQ individuals are robust and accessible. This includes:

- **Community Centers:** Establishing LGBTQ community centers that provide safe spaces for individuals to gather, share experiences, and access resources.

- **Mental Health Support:** Creating mental health programs tailored to the unique challenges faced by LGBTQ individuals, including trauma-informed care and peer support groups.

These support networks not only provide immediate assistance but also foster a sense of belonging and solidarity within the community.

## Intersectionality in Advocacy

Wai Wai Nu's vision is deeply rooted in the understanding of intersectionality, recognizing that LGBTQ individuals often face multiple layers of discrimination based on ethnicity, gender, and socio-economic status. Her advocacy work seeks to:

- **Highlight Diverse Voices:** Amplifying the voices of LGBTQ individuals from various ethnic backgrounds to ensure that advocacy efforts are inclusive and representative.

- **Collaborate Across Movements:** Building alliances with other social justice movements, such as women's rights and ethnic minority rights, to create a united front against discrimination.

This intersectional approach not only strengthens the LGBTQ rights movement but also contributes to broader societal change.

## Global Solidarity and Influence

Wai Wai Nu envisions a future where Myanmar's LGBTQ rights movement is part of a global network of solidarity. She believes that:

+ **Sharing Stories:** Engaging with international media and participating in global LGBTQ conferences can help share Myanmar's unique challenges and triumphs, fostering understanding and support worldwide.

+ **Collaborative Advocacy:** Partnering with international LGBTQ organizations can enhance resources and strategies for local activism, ensuring that the voices of Myanmar's LGBTQ community are heard on the global stage.

This global perspective not only provides support but also brings attention to the specific issues faced by LGBTQ individuals in Myanmar, encouraging international pressure for change.

## Conclusion: A Vision of Hope

Ultimately, Wai Wai Nu's vision for the future is one of hope and resilience. By addressing the root causes of discrimination, empowering individuals through education, advocating for legal reforms, building supportive networks, and fostering global solidarity, she believes that a brighter future is possible for LGBTQ individuals in Myanmar. Her vision is not just about achieving rights; it is about creating a society where everyone can live authentically and with dignity, free from fear and prejudice.

In this vision, the journey of activism is continuous, requiring commitment, courage, and collaboration. Wai Wai Nu stands as a beacon of hope, demonstrating that change is not only possible but essential for the well-being of all individuals, regardless of their sexual orientation or gender identity. The future she envisions is one where love, acceptance, and equality reign supreme, paving the way for generations to come.

# Index

9 781779 695871